ɑɒ aquapre

C000186006

Scapa Flow
DIVE GUIDE

Lawson Wood

EXPLORER SERIES

Copyright © 2008 Lawson Wood

www.lawsonwood.com

The right of Lawson Wood to be identified as the author of this work has
been asserted in accordance with the Copyright Designs and Patents Act,1988.

All rights reserved.

This book is sold subject to the condition that it shall not, by way of trade or otherwise, be
lent, resold, hired out, or otherwise circulated without the publisher's prior consent in any
form of binding or cover other than that in which it is published and without a similar
condition including this condition being imposed on the subsequent purchaser.

An AquaPress Book

Published and distributed from AquaPress

25 Farriers Way

Temple Farm Industrial Estate

Southend-on-Sea

Essex, SS2 5RY

United Kingdom

www.aquapress.co.uk

First Published 2007

Second Edition 2008

AquaPress and the AquaPress Logo are Trademarks of AquaPress.
AquaPress © 2008. All rights reserved.

A CIP catalogue record for this book is available from the British Library.

Although the author and publisher have made every effort to ensure that the information in
this book was correct at the time of going to press, they accept no responsibility for any loss,
injury or inconvenience sustained by any person using this book.

For information on all other AquaPress titles visit www.aquapress.co.uk

ISBN: 1-905492-11-1

Epitaph

The photographs on page 40 and 44/45 are of my friend and diving buddy George Hendry.
George sadly died on 11th August 2007 enjoying his passion, the shipwrecks of Scapa Flow.

UNITED KINGDOM

Orkney Islands

Scapa Flow

Inverness

Aberdeen

Rosyth

Atlantic Ocean

St. Abbs

Glasgow

Edinburgh

North Sea

Newcastle

Manchester

London

Dover

English Channel

Contents

The German Fleet at rest in Scapa Flow, shortly before they were scuttled.

Foreword

Our tale opens in the First World War, when Scapa flow was chosen as the base for the British Grand Fleet - and one day in 1914, almost out of the blue, with precision planning, 70,000 men in 96 ships arrived in Orkney, to the astonishment and utter unpreparedness of the islanders. When I tell you that the total population of the islands today is less than 20,000, you will understand the impact. At the victorious end of the First World War, when the German High Seas Fleet entered Scapa Flow under very different circumstances - to be interned under the terms of the Armistice, history was to take another dramatic turn. 74 German ships, including its best 11 battleships and 5 battlecruisers, were anchored in a great semi-circle around the island of Cava for months. As time went by and the Allies bickered among themselves about the fate of the ships, the skeleton German crews were heartily disgruntled. The final straw came when they heard the terms of the Treaty of Versailles, which allowed the Germany of a peaceful future only a tiny fleet - 6 battleships and no submarines.

So it was that, on Midsummers Day 1919, when the British fleet was out on exercises, Admiral von Reuter gave the order to his men to open the sea-cocks. Most of the fleet was scuttled; some ships were beached - all to the astonishment of a party of Orcadian schoolchildren who watched the crews whooping and shouting for joy as they made off in small boats.

This event is the largest intentional sinking in worldwide naval history. The recovery of most of the fleet, between 1923 and 1939, was one of the most outstanding marine salvage feats of all time. For almost all the ships were raised and towed south to the Firth of Forth and broken up at Rosyth for scrap iron. Seven massive wrecks of warships survive on the flat, muddy seabed - up to 25,000 tons and over 200m in length at a depth of 30-50m.

Sports diving is seriously big business in Orkney and has been for many years. Scapa Flow is one of the most popular dive sites in Europe. Recreational diving alone contributes well over £1,000,000 a year to Orkney's economy, with up to 3,000 divers making almost 30,000 dives a year, about 60% of them on what's left of the German High Seas Fleet and that's a conservative estimate. It translates to thousands of divers needing accommodation, transport, shops and equipment. Spending time and money in the islands; and thousands being carried by Orkney dive boat operators and others, whose livelihoods depend on the diving industry.

In the story of the German High Seas Fleet at Scapa Flow, we have a microcosm of the changing approach to historic wrecks and the way we as a society value them:

First, they were seen as weapons of mass destruction (1918-21);

Then as a salvage resource (1923-39);

Then an unrestricted diving amenity (1960s onwards);

Finally, as national historic and archaeological assets, worthy of protection by law.

As for the remaining seven wrecks, scheduling should help to ensure that they survive as intact as possible, for as long as possible, for the enjoyment and opportunities they offer to succeeding generations of Orcadians, dive boat operators - and the vast majority of responsible divers. This book by Lawson Wood is a worthy account of the ships, their history, their importance and their place in the grander scheme of things. Readers can also learn about the importance of the Blockships, the sad fate of three British Battleships now designated War Graves and of course the prolific marine life which abounds in these northern waters.

Bobby Forbes, SULA Diving, Orkney.

Stromness Harbour has changed little over the last 100 years.

Orkney Introduction

Separated by only the six mile wide channel of the Pentland Firth, Orkney has some 90 islands, 18 of which are inhabited. Apart from the island of Hoy, Orkney consists of fairly flat and rolling farmland interspersed with wetlands and meadows. On the same latitude as southern Greenland, Alaska and Leningrad (all places which are synonymous with extreme cold), Orkney is bathed in the warm waters of the North Atlantic Drift which first started out as the Gulf Stream in the Caribbean. Hence, winters may be wet, but they are generally mild and whilst the islands are inevitable windy, the locals don't complain much!

Created by submergence, the islands of Orkney give the impression of tipping westwards into the sea and when you stand on the cliffs at Yesnaby it is remarkably evident. There are great sea stacks, arches, caves and caverns all around the coast, some of which are world famous such as the Old Man of Hoy. The total land mass is around 603.5 sq.km (375 square miles) and the coastline is deeply indented. The northern isles promise adventure and are steeped in a history that is quite unrivalled in the western hemisphere.

When you travel around Orkney you cannot help but notice the standing stones and ancient stone rings which predate the Norsemen as far back as Stone Age, Bronze and Iron Ages and the Picts. Although very little is known of these early times, other than the monuments themselves, detailed history of the Norse Occupation was not committed to paper until the 13th century in Iceland. The Orkneyinga Saga tells the tale of the Earl's of Orkney and the occupation of the islands.

Scapa Flow was the base of the British Naval Fleet over several generations and indeed had served the nation well during the Napoleonic War and the American War of Independence. Early photographs show the home fleet at anchor, their perfectly straight and regimented rows of dreadnoughts, battleships and cruisers, bedecked in bunting and firing a 'Royal Salute'.

Orkney had the almost perfect naval base with calm sheltered waters surrounded by islands, creating a deep natural harbour first named by the Vikings. The name Scapa is from the ancient Norse word *skalpr* meaning sword scabbard or from *skalpei* which can mean ship or isthmus, depending on the grammar in the description. Flow has it's roots from *floi* or *fljot* which is a derivation of fjiord meaning 'large body of water'; therefore a basic translation of Scapa Flow's name was a simple description for 'a large sheltered body of water with protected islands and sheltered access for ships to be beached and repaired'. Now *'Skalpei Floi'* is still a centre for shipping commerce with a massive oil and gas terminal on the Island of Flotta. Scapa Flow has risen to become one of the top scuba diving destinations in the world with world class wrecks dating from the world's last great conflicts.

There is also another interesting derivation which comes from WWI. The slang word 'scarper' means to 'run away' and this derives from an Italian word 'scappare' meaning 'to escape'. The word became very popular amongst the Cockney squaddies who were on duty in Orkney and used their rhyming slang for Scapa Flow meaning 'go!'

Graeme Spence, Maritime Surveyor to the Admiralty said in 1812 ...

"the art of Man, aided by all the Dykes, Sea Walls or Break-Waters that could possibly be built could not have contained a better Roadstead than the peculiar situation and extent of the South Isles of Orkney have made Scapa Flow ... from whatever point the Wind blows a Vessel in Scapa Flow may make a fair wind of it out to free sea... a property which no other Roadstead I know of possesses, and without waiting for Tide on which account it may be called the Key to both Oceans".

Considered by many to be impregnable to attack, the bay of Scapa Flow covers some 190sq.km (120 square miles) and is now almost totally landlocked with Mainland to the north, the islands of Hoy and Flotta to the south and west and to the south and east the Churchill Barriers link the islands of Lamb Holm, Glims Holm, Burray and South Ronaldsay to the Mainland. This makes for some relatively calm waters for most of the year.

The wrecks are actually dotted all over Scapa Flow, with Blockships found in the extreme east and west of the Flow and the German light cruisers and battleships found roughly in the centre of Scapa Flow, arranged in a horseshoe shape near a rocky pinnacle called the Barrel of Butter. However because the tidal streams which used to pass through the sound have been altered due to the barriers, Scapa Flow just isn't as clear as you would like it to be as the particulate in the water tends to stay in suspension for quite long periods, particularly after the algae blooms in the Spring and Autumn.

Scapa Flow is undoubtedly the best wreck diving in Europe and certainly ranks in the top five of the World. There is more wreckage in Scapa Flow than any other location on the planet. This deep, formidable, cold, natural harbour has served the warring nations' fleets since the time of the Vikings; the Knights of St. John; the Spanish Armada and the American War of Independence. Scapa Bay was also the rendezvous point for merchant ships enroute to the Baltic during the Napoleonic Wars from 1789 to 1815.

At present and visited regularly by divers are 3 German battleships; 4 battleship debris sites; 4 light cruisers; 1 light cruiser debris site; 5 torpedo boats (small destroyers); a WWII destroyer (F2); 1 German submarine, UB116; 47 large sections of remains and salvor's equipment; 17 large diveable blockships out of a total of 43 sunk; a further 11 unidentified wrecks; another 15 known wrecks including several barges and many other bits of wreckage as yet unidentified including four aircraft. Finally, there are also 2 British battleships (the *Vanguard* and the *Royal Oak*). It should be pointed out that in the above list, the *Vanguard* and the *Royal Oak* are both classed as war graves and no unauthorised diving is permitted on them. For the most part, all of the diving is in open water, jumping off the side of a boat and swimming down a shot line in generally poor visibility in dark water. The remaining German shipwrecks of Scapa Flow have been deteriorating steadily since 1919 and extreme caution should be exercised when approaching these wrecks.

Over the years a certain unfounded and unjust notoriety has evolved when talking about diving on the wrecks of Scapa Flow. This is perhaps due to the impression that some novice divers think that wreck diving is only deep and dangerous and that many divers are lost on these wrecks yearly due to the hazardous conditions. They may also feel that Scapa Flow diving is also only for 'macho' experienced divers. Yes, divers have lost their lives here over the years, but this is the same for every popular diving destination and not all of the losses are regarded as diving incidents. Nowadays, divers are more informed, better trained and have the very latest diving computers to guide them through the complicated variables of multi-level and mixed gas diving.

Many divers still assume that you can only explore the German Fleet wrecks using nitrox, trimix or rebreathers and that all of them should be treated as decompression dives, only to be dived by super-qualified divers. Diving in Scapa Flow can be as simple or as complicated as you want to make it. Novice divers can have a great diving holiday in Scapa Flow and indeed many visitors gain their first diving qualification through the excellent diving schools on the island. The shallowest part of the *Karlsruhe II* is in only 15m (50ft) and the seabed is less than 26m (85ft) deep. All of the Motor Torpedo Boats and Blockships are in less than 18m (60ft), with many in less than 9m (30ft) and are quite possibly some of the best shallow shipwrecks in the world: therefore virtually all the Blockships and German light cruisers are achievable for novice divers (under supervision). A diving holiday in Scapa Flow is realistic for novice divers, as the diving on offer goes beyond mere opinion, novice divers are able to dive alongside those super-qualified, mixed gas and rebreather divers on over 70% of the same shipwrecks.

The Flag of the German Imperial Navy

German High Seas Fleet

To safeguard Germany's colonial expansion, Kaiser Wilhelm II was persuaded by Alfred Tirpitz that the way forward for a unified Germany was to amalgamate the navy's two components, the German Navy Office with the High Command. His ambition led to his appointment as State Secretary of the Imperial Navy Office in 1897. Plans were quickly drawn up to increase the might of Germany's navy and once started would continue to develop as the industrial capacity increased. It was recognised that they would never have the time to amass a fleet to match the numbers and capacity of the British fleet, however it was clear that military advancements on both sides would ultimately precipitate a head on clash. The Anglo/German arms race culminated in the massive Dreadnought type of battleship and battlecruiser design. It was this type of craft which inevitably heralded the First World War.

When war finally broke out on the 4th August 1914, Admiral Sir John Jellico took over command of the Grand Fleet from their base headquarters near Scapa Pier. Jellico immediately recognised the vulnerability of Scapa Flow when their "impenetrable" defences were breached by the U-Boat U-18 in November of that year. He quickly took control of the situation and transferred the base headquarters to Longhope. He then installed a complete new system of defences including the placing of Blockships at five of the approaches to Scapa Flow. With these security measures in place, Scapa Flow became the major training ground for all of the naval fleet before engaging in active duty in the Atlantic and North Sea.

Now at war with Germany, the allies continued in their preparations for active duty. It was clear that Germany was going to make a move into the North Sea from their bases in Germany and both the Grand Fleet and Atlantic Fleet sat in readiness. Early reconnaissance indicated that the German High Seas Fleet had finally put to sea on 30th May 1916 and were making their way

Left: A Diver on the bows of the Cöln II

towards the British naval bases. Admiral Jellico left Scapa Flow on his flagship *HMS Iron Duke* with a fleet comprising of 16 battleships. 3 battle cruisers, 4 armoured cruisers, 5 light cruisers and 44 destroyers. Admiral Sir David Beatty headed the second spear of the attacking fleet and their combined forces greatly outnumbered the German Fleet by 144 ships to 99. The two fleets met on 31st May, 1916 and the Battle of Jutland raged. Their respective commanders, Admiral Jellico and Admiral Scheer handled the manoeuvres of their fleets with great skill, but they met late on in the day and subsequent fires and heavy smoke quickly reduced the visibility. Twenty-five ships were lost from both sides and although the outcome was indecisive, both sides claimed moral victories. Admiral Scheer made use of the reduced visibility that day and he signalled the German fleet to break off the engagement and head for home. The German High Seas Fleet would never see action of such force again for the rest of the war.

Germany's High Seas Battle Fleet languished at their naval bases at Keil and Wilhelmshaven and the crew quickly became demoralised. Supplies were poor, wages had not been paid and the peace negotiations were incredibly slow in deciding their fate. Communist sympathisers under the control of the Soviet of Workers, Soldiers and Sailors had infiltrated the ranks and dissent quickly followed. Germany's ports were now blockaded by the British Navy and when the German Fleet was ordered to assemble and break through the blockade, a full scale mutiny broke out during October 1918. The mutinous crews took control of both naval bases and this ultimately provoked the abdication of the Kaiser and the formation of a new government.

The British poking fun at the inactivity of the German Navy

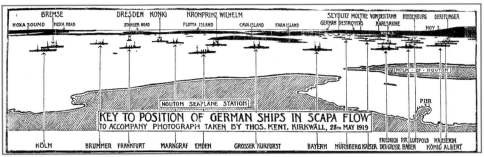

A contemporary drawing indicating the postition of the German High Seas Battle Fleet.

Germany's land forces had been crushed and their leaders were now engaged in the terms of surrender. However the German High Seas Battle Fleet had survived the war relatively intact. It had been constructed at enormous cost and was now used as a pawn in the peace negotiations. The German Navy posed a significant threat to the allies, should peace negotiations break down over the terms of the surrender. Amidst all this dissent, there is great speculation, in one of the last military actions in the Great War over the sinking of another German U Boat in Scapa Flow, the *UB116* on 28th October. When the submarine wreckage was inspected a few days after, the 'tin-openers' only found drowned men wearing officers uniforms and suitcases filled with personal items and civilian clothes. Perhaps these brave souls had already seen the end of the war and were coming to surrender.

The direct result of the interim peace negotiations of the armistice resulted in the agreement to inter the German Fleet in exchange for the lifting of the blockade until a deal could be struck between the Allies and the new German Government. The fleet's ammunition and breech blocks were removed in the naval bases and most of the crew were removed from active duty. Now with only a skeleton crew, the entire German Naval Fleet set sail once more and congregated in the Firth of Forth on 21st November 1918. There they were met by the new British Commander-in-Chief, Admiral Sir David Beatty on board his flagship *HMS Queen Elizabeth* and Vice-Admiral Madden on board *HMS Revenge*. First contact between the two fleets took place at 09.40 hours that day and the *Frederich der Grosse* led a full compliment of a further ten battleships; five battle cruisers; eight light cruisers; fifty destroyers and motor torpedo boats. All of the remaining submarine companies were transferred to Harwich.

From there, the assembled fleets made their way slowly north to Scapa Flow where the base of the home fleet would play host to one of the most amazing sights ever to be seen at sea. On 23rd November 1918, the Orcadians woke up to witness the greatest naval spectacle ever seen on the planet.

Almost the entire naval fleets of both Germany and the United Kingdom were at anchor in Scapa Flow.

Message from the Board of Admiralty:

"The Board of Admiralty desirento express to the officers and men of the Royal Navy and Royal Marines on completion of their great work their congratulations on a triumph to which history knows no parallel.

The surrender of the German Fleet, accomplished without shock of battle, will remain for all time the example of the wonderful silence and sureness with which Sea Power attains its end.

The world recognises that this consummation is due to the steadfastness with which the navy has maintained its pressure on the enemy through more than four years of war, a pressure exerted no less insistently during the long monotony of waiting than in the rare opportunities of attack." *

By mid December, the 20,000 German sailors who had manned the High Seas Fleet to sail to Scapa Flow were reduced to a skeleton crew of around 4,800 comprising of a caretaker crew of 200 per battlecruiser, 175 per battleship, 80 per light cruiser and 20 per destroyer (torpedo-boat) leaving a nominal total of 4,565 plus 250 officers and warrant officers, although the exact actual figures are thought to be higher.

This was considerably more than the British thought necessary but for once the German view prevailed.

These numbers were further reduced in early June to Royal Navy caretaker levels, 75 per battlecruiser, 60 per battleship, 30 per light

*Credit: National Archives ADM/116/1825-212971

cruiser and whomever was necessary for the destroyers, in total around 1820 officers and men.

von Reuter had his way and included 150 dissidents and trouble-makers in the last repatriation and transferred his flag to the *Emden* which was much warmer than his previous quarters.

von Reuter was utterly convinced that the Allies would take control of his fleet, should peace negotiations break down and he apparently took it upon himself to defy the world, the Allies and his Nation to save them from further ignominy.

His dilemma was further exacerbated by mutinous crews, lack of supplies and freezing cold vessels.

He knew that the allied powers were looking at the German Fleet as the spoils of war and his real fear was that the fleet would be taken and used in action against his country.

He said:

"It is my intention to sink the ships only if the enemy should attempt to obtain possession of them without the assent of our Government.

Should our Government agree in the peace terms to the surrender of the ships, then the ships will be handed over, to the lasting disgrace of those who have placed us in this position. "

As early as 1st June 1919, von Reuter had made plans for the scuttling of the fleet.

He sent his instructions to all his trustworthy

officers on each of the German ships by British naval escort ship!

Although no direct contact was allowed between each of the ships or with Germany, we can only surmise that this was not the case. By the early 1900's, all British shipping were fitted with Wireless Telegraphy equipment, supplied by the Marconi Telegraph Co. To keep pace with demand they found it necessary to sub-contract work. The Glasgow firm of McGeogh produced the displayed Morse key in 1907.

The large key was fitted to the German Battleship *Grosser Kurfurst* in 1912. When the German fleet was interned at Scapa Flow at the end of WW1, all Morse keys were supposedly removed to prevent inter-ship communication. However a morse key had remained secreted aboard and sank to the bottom of Scapa Flow when the scuttles were opened on 21 June 1919. It was subsequently recovered in a salvage operation conducted by Metal Industries Ltd. in 1937. One can only assume that if there was one Morse key, there were more and indeed another morse key was found on the V78.

von Reuter informed all of his officers and trustworthy companions (in code), that the men on board were to ready the seacocks and prepare their torpedo tubes for flooding and all watertight doors; hatchways; ventilators and skuttles were to be rendered useless.

He had read in a copy of the Timers newspaper (which was several days old) details of the peace agreements and decided to make preparations to sink the fleet.

Sadly he acted on information that was not only out of date, it was also wrong.

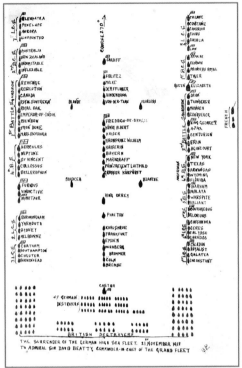

Sailing order posted of the fleets

Taking advantage of the reduced numbers of men, he knew that it would only take a minimal amount of work to prepare the fleet for sinking should the right time and opportunity arise.

Keeping a keen sailors eye on the British Home Fleet, he learned that the British Fleet was due to leave Scapa Bay on torpedo firing exercises early on the morning of June 16th, 1919.

True to form, the First Battle Squadron, led by Vice Admiral, Sir Sydney Freemantle left Scapa Flow at 9 a.m.

They left behind only a small caretaking fleet comprising of the *Westcott*, her sistership *Walpole* (which was temporarily out of service), the *Vespa*, and her sistership the *Vega*, also under repairs, the depot ship *Sandhurst* and various guard drifters and boom defence trawlers.

At 10:30am von Reuter ordered the following signal to be hoisted: 'Group Writing. First Paragraph Eleven, Confirm. Chief I.V.'

This was the prearranged code for immediate scuttle.

The controlled suicide of the entire fleet had begun and it took over an hour before his message was relayed around the entire fleet and his signal acknowledged.

Stopcocks were opened and rendered unworkable, shifting keys and spanners were thrown overboard and once the scuttling started the only way to possibly stop the boats from sinking was to tow them and beach them in shallow water.

The first of the German Fleet to sink after the order to scuttle was issued was the Friedrich der Grosse - the former flagship of the Jutland Fleet. This battleship sank beneath the surface at 12:16pm. The Bayern sunk stern first then rolled over, the Seydlitz also rolled over onto her side as did the Moltke, their heavy guns forcing them over as they went down. Those in shallower water like the Hindenburg sank on an even keel with all of her superstructure still out of the water. Soon the surface of Scapa Flow was awash with oil and other loose debris including huge amounts of paperwork, the German Fleet finally ridding itself of all propaganda and official orders.

Rear Admiral R.J. Prendergast on the flagship HMS Victorious (which was little more than a workshop and dockyard ship with no armaments) had already seen that the German ships were flying their ensigns and battle flags contrary to standing orders and immediately recalled the British Fleet from exercise and called in whatever ships and men that were still on duty in Scapa Flow.

Their orders were simple enough – to order the German sailors responsible to close the seacocks and lower their battle flags and to stop the sinking of the fleet by any means possible.

By 2pm the British First Battle Squadron was charging back to try valiantly to stop any further sinking. Boatloads of German sailors were crying for help, most were picked up by the remaining force in Scapa, however many landed on the nearby islands.

Over 400,000 tons of modern warships were sunk that day, the largest loss of shipping in a single day in history.

Publicly the British Admiralty were outraged but in private there was a sense of relief that the problem of what to do with the fleet was now over.

Many people still believe in the complicity of the British Government with the German Fleet High Command, speculating that the British knew all about the orders and rather than let the German Fleet be dispersed amongst her allies (including Japan, Italy, France, Australia and the United States) they decided to ignore the sinking orders which von Reuter had actually sent out to his fleet by British Dispatch Boat.

The coincidence of the entire British Fleet leaving the very morning of the sinking, may just have been good planning by von Reuter.

However considerable efforts were made by

British Intelligence to prove that the scuttling had been authorised by Berlin but they never found any proof.

von Reuter took the blame entirely on himself and was declared a hero by his nation that day.

Sadly two German officers and six men were killed in the skirmishes that followed, plus another five sailors were wounded. The 1820 officers and men were now treated as Prisoners of War and were gradually repatriated to Germany.

Matters arising from the Scapa Flow incident concluded that the British Admiralty were firmly of the opinion that the German Government be held entirely responsible for the violation of the terms of the Armistice, involved in the sinking of the ships.

The British Admiralty demanded that some form of reparation be made by the German Government and that the following should be claimed for:

A   The Loss of the Ships

B   The cost of the Salvage of the Ships

C   The cost of surveying the anchorage, buoying the wrecks etc.

D   Any subsequent expenses incurred eg. In clearing the anchorage of wrecks.

E   Reparation should be in kind, and the only evident forms which this reparation can take are:-

(i)   Warships

(ii)   Floating docks; cranes and harbour craft of all kinds which are left to Germany under the Peace Treaty.

The British Admiralty also recovered 34,642 Marks and 20 pfennigs of Government money and 7,444 Marks in private money from the sunken ships during the first salvage operations. It so happened that in one fell swoop, not only did the British Government get rid of the German High Seas Battle Fleet, they also gained all of the necessary equipment which would be needed for the salvage of the craft.

Naval salvage advisors arrived on 24th June and after a thorough investigation declared that the remaining sunken fleet could not be viably salvaged and that they should be buoyed as navigational hazards.

However, peace reigned, the ships lay rusting, mainly on the seabed and many locals became quite skilled at that 'diving lark' to salvage what they could from the stricken vessels.

Many ships ran aground on the hulks, others became snagged on cables etc and floating debris became a very real hazard in Scapa Flow.

Virtually all of the wildlife around the shores had been killed off by the leaking oil and locals were becoming concerned that their livelihoods were in danger, now that there was a mass exodus of military personnel from Orkney.

As the post-war industries became rekindled, the need for scrap metal rose and gradually interest was turned to Scapa Flow, which from all accounts was stuffed full of scrap metal.

Ernest Frank Guelph Cox, born in Wolverhampton would be the man to rise to the challenge of buying a navy for scrap.

Credit: National Archives ADM/116/1825-212971

Salvage diver and work crew at Scapa Flow

Salvaging the German Fleet

The first local salvage company was formed in 1922 and the Stromness Salvage Company purchased the destroyer *G 89* which had been beached on Cava. They managed to refloat the vessel, tow her to Stromness and scrap her. They eventually sold the still floating hulk to Cox and Danks in 1928 for £50.00 who later used her as a counterweight in the salvage of the Seydlitz.

The United Kingdom Salvage Company of Glasgow in conjunction with Mr. J.W. Robertson formed the Scapa Flow Salvage and Shipbreaking Company in 1923 and initially bought four destroyers. They had planned to raise the destroyers by steel hawsers strung across two concrete barges, tow the ships to shallow water, let the tide go out and repeat the process until the ship could be pumped dry. However before they could even get their first ship lifted, another rival operation moved in to Scapa Flow.

Frank Cox's company, Cox and Danks was already a very successful scrap iron company and were involved in clearing up Britain's ailing railway engines. He saw the opportunity in Scapa Flow where everyone else before had refused to believe that the great ships could be salvaged, Cox struck on an idea that not only could he salvage the ships, he could actually refloat them and tow them to the breaking yards at Rosyth on the northern shore of the Firth of Forth. He acquired one of the floating docks which was part of the German reparation costs which could raise 3,000 tons in a dead lift, perfect for the Motor Torpedo Boats and smaller Destroyers which only weighed between 800-1,500 tons each. His initial purchase was twenty-six destroyers and two battleships from the Admiralty in 1924. With two ex-Admiralty tugs, the *Ferrodanks* and the *Sinodian,* as well as the German dry dock, he outfitted the vessels with £40,000 of equipment including compressors, generators, railway tracks, a small train, crane jibs, workshops, hawsers, winches, standard diving equipment and men. After traveling the 1126km (700 miles) to Scapa

Left: The upturned hull of one of the battlecruisers on her way to the Rosyth breaking yards

Guns of salvaged German Battleship

the *Hindenburg* in 1927, he tried again and managed to float her onto an even keel on 22nd July 1930. Unlike all of the other capital ships, he floated the *Hindenburg* south to the breaking yards, upright and relatively intact. His next conquest was to raise the *Prinzregent Luitpold* on 9th July 1931.

From his early beginning in March 1924 and over the next eight years, he raised two battleships, four battlecruisers, one light cruiser and 25 destroyers/motor torpedo boats by pumping compressed air into the hulls. His first ship only took ten days to raise but before long, as one observer recorded, "he fished up ships almost as easily as an angler winds in salmon". By 1932, the price of scrap was starting to fall and Frank Cox decided to cut any future losses and sold his company to the Alloa Shipbreaking Company which had been shifting his scrap, they renamed their new salvage company Metal Industries.

Metal Industries raised their first ship by the compressed air method on 5th September 1934. They went on to raise the 28,000 ton *Bayern* and even managed to float the *König Albert* from 41m (138ft). They continued very successfully to raise the 25,000 ton *Kaiserin;* the 25,000 ton *Frederich der Grosse* (reaching an all time scrap record of £150,000. (Interestingly, the *Frederich der Grosse* was shipped south to Rosyth along with part of the German dry dock and the salvage vessel *Metinda* which had sunk in a gale and was underwater for six months. She was salvaged at the same time and actually sailed under her own steam to the Forth where she was refitted and sent back up to Scapa Flow.) Metal Industries also raised the

he re-assessed the state of the remaining wrecks and made a further purchase of the battleships *Moltke* and *von der Tann*, the battlecruisers *Kaiser* and *Prinzregent Luitpold* and the light cruiser *Bremse*.

Employing the same methodology that Mr. Robertson was going to use, they raised a few of the lighter destroyers. After further consultation with Naval architects he hit upon the revolutionary plan to seal all of the holes in the deeper battleships, pump them full of air and basically float them off the bottom. Huge towers were constructed and attached onto the ship's hulls containing pressure locks. The divers then climbed down the towers, blew out the water from the towers with the use of compressed air and cut through into the interior of the ship. The first ship to be raised by this method was the *Moltke* on 10th June 1927. At 22,640 tons, this was the largest ship ever raised off the seabed at the time. She was beached on Cava, towed to Lyness and all of the ship's heavy machinery and guns were removed in preparation for the long tow south to Rosyth. (Ironically this was done by a German salvage company!) The 25,000 ton *Seydlitz* was raised the same way on 3rd November that same year, followed by the *Kaiser* on 20th March 1929. After spending £30,000 in a failed bid to raise

25,000 ton *Grosser Kurfürst* and finally the *Derfflinger* at 28,000tons. The *Derfflinger* was the largest ship ever raised from the deepest water, 45m (150ft).

It should be noted here that not only were Metal Industries raising the sunken German Fleet, there were many delays in this task, not simply because of the engineering logistics involved, it was because they were employed in other diversions in and around Scapa Flow, primarily for the British Admiralty. Metal Industries summary of work from 3rd September 1939 to 15th August 1945 was incredible and consisted of the following:-

Wrecks dispersed	4
Blockships prepared and sunk	22
Net and wire defences run and maintained	4
Temporary hull repairs	144
Propellers cleared	435
Ship inlets cleared	950
Anchors and cables recovered	147
Moorings cleared	18
Diving surveys	312
Underwater cutting and welding	9
D.C. Ranges repaired	16
Berths cleared	6
Objects recovered	133
Repairs to Allied vessels	185
Additional repair jobs to hulls, engines, boilers and auxiliary machinery etc.	8487

Metal Industries also salvaged a further 64 boom vessels, tugs and drifters; 177 motor boats and miscellaneous small craft; five naval aircraft; eight torpedoes (including the electrically propelled torpedo remains which sunk the *Royal Oak*); nine Royal Fleet Auxiliary War Department vessels; two flying boats; a helicopter and a narrow gauge locomotive all from depths up to and exceeding 36m (120ft).*

Metal Industries continued working in Scapa Flow until March 1947 when they moved to Faslane in Loch Long. They sold their interests

The ships were salvaged by pumping compressed air into their hulls

to one of their former salvage divers, Arthur Nundy in 1956. Nundy Marine Metals continued to work the German Fleet, unfortunately for the state of the remaining ships and for the future enjoyment of visiting divers, Nundy simply blasted his way into the interior of the ships and removed all of the easy bits. He worked diligently at reducing the ships systematically up until 1972 when he sold his salvage rights to Scapa Flow Salvage. Scapa Flow Salvage continued to work the lower and more difficult parts of the ships until the work became no longer viable. Now completely protected, only seven of the original battleships and light cruisers have been left on the seabed, as well as a scattering of remains of motor torpedo boats and destroyers.

* Credit: Public Record Office, National Archives ADM 1/8428/216; ADM 116/5790; ADM 116/56319

COURTESY OF LESLEY ORSON

The Ferry MV Hamnavoe berthed at Stromness harbour

Travelling to & staying in Scapa

GETTING TO ORKNEY

Orkney lies just a short six miles from the Scottish mainland and the principal route to the Isles is by Ferry from Scrabster. Scrabster is the small village, fishing port and ferry terminal just north of Thurso and can be reached by car along the A9 which extends from Edinburgh, across the Forth Road Bridge, up through the Scottish Highlands and onwards through Inverness. Most people take a beak at Inverness and all of the required facilities can be found almost next door to each other:- Restaurant and toilets, petrol station and even a "Kwik-Fit" for any unforeseen repairs.

The ferry from Scrabster to Stromness in Orkney is currently operated by Northlink Ferries, who also operate the ferry from Aberdeen to Kirkwall and a link on to Lerwick in the Shetland Islands. The ultra modern *MV Hamnavoe* runs the Scrabster to Stromness link and return and has three sailings per day midweek and two sailings per day over the weekend. Sailing time is 2½ hours. There are only four sailing per week from Aberdeen to Kirkwall on Tuesday, Thursday, Saturday and Sunday and only one trip per day, the journey time is 6 hours from Aberdeen and 7½ hours return. Many people actually prefer the Aberdeen trip, as the journey time by Road from Edinburgh is only around three hours due to the continuous dual carriageway and motorway link, followed by a six hour ferry crossing. The A9 north from Perth to Caithness, however scenic it is, is not exactly the best run in the world and may take you eight hours by road from Edinburgh.

Northlink Ferry reservations: Tel: (0845) 6000 449; www.northlinkferries.co.uk

From May to September, there are a further two ferries from Gills Bay to St Margarets Hope on

Left: The author by one of the Standing Stones of Stenness

South Ronaldsay and from John O'Groats to Burwick also on South Ronaldsay. These ferry links are serviced by the Orkney Bus and can be ticketed from Inverness to Kirkwall. The Gills Bay to St. Margaret's Hope route takes one hour and runs three times per day. It also has a few winter sailings and is serviced by Pentland Ferries Ltd. The John O'Groats to Burwick route is for passengers only and is operated by John O'Groats Ferries. Bookings in advance are essential as these are only small ferries. Whilst on Mainland Orkney, you may want to explore some of the outer islands and there are regular daily services to all of the inhabited northern islands. These are operated by Orkney Ferries Ltd.

Pentland Ferries Ltd. Tel: (01856) 831226; www.pentlandferries.co.uk

John O'Groats Ferries., Tel: (01955) 611353; www.jogferry.co.uk

Orkney Ferries Ltd. Tel: (01856) 872044; www.orkneyferries.co.uk

By air, Kirkwall is 90 minutes from Edinburgh or Glasgow, 45 minutes from Aberdeen and a mere half hour from Inverness. British Airways, franchised to Loganair, operate flights from all of the above airports, all of which have excellent UK connections. Glasgow, Edinburgh and Aberdeen also have good international connections and if you are flying in from Ireland or the USA, you can fly direct to Glasgow or Prestwick Airports. On approaching Kirkwall Airport, you will get a superb view of Scapa Flow, Orkney Mainland and all the surrounding islands.

British Airways Tel: (0870) 850 9850; www.ba.com

Kirkwall Airport Information Desk Tel: (01856) 886210.

By Train you can travel to Thurso, where a bus connects to the ferry at Scrabster, or Aberdeen where the railway station is near to the harbour area. There is also a coach connection from Inverness and Wick to Gills Bay. By coach you can go either to Scrabster or to John O'Groats (but remember that the John O'Groats route is a summer, passenger only- service).

Scotrail Railways Ltd. Tel: (08457) 484950; www.scotrail.co.uk.

Orkney Coaches, Tel: (01856) 870555; www.rapsons.co.uk.

Scottish Citylink Coaches Ltd. Tel: (08705) 505050; www.citylink.co.uk

WHERE TO STAY IN ORKNEY

There is a wide range of accommodation to suit all pockets, but most divers generally stay in Stromness and its environs as virtually all of the day dive boats operate out of Stromness Harbour and leave around 7.30–8.00 am each day. Unless you have a car, it is generally best to stay close by the dive boats or with a dive boat operator. A few of the diving companies offer live-aboard accommodation and this allows for a greater range of exploration, as most boats will actually venture out of Scapa Flow (given the chance) to give you some of the most scenic diving you are likely to encounter anywhere. A full list of accommodation can be found in the Orkney Tourist Board brochures. Tel: (01856) 872856; www.visitorkney.com

Coastline viewed from Yesnaby

WHAT TO SEE IN ORKNEY

Whilst this publication is aimed at divers, there is so much more to see and do whilst in Orkney. For those not staying on a live-aboard dive boat for the week and are coming in after each day's diving, there is always plenty to see fairly close by to Stromness harbour. Dive boats usually return around 4.30 – 5.30pm and this gives ample time to do some mainland exploring. The tourism product is an amalgam of specialist interests including history; archaeology; ornithology; natural history; trout fishing; sub-aqua diving; sea angling and yachting.

- Orkney is the richest historic area in Britian with over 1,000 recorded sites.

- There are ten RSPB Nature Reserves.

- Scapa Flow is reputably the best single dive area in Europe with more wrecks here than in any other place.

- The islands are the most visited Cruise Liner port in Scotland.

- The largest example of fish species are caught in these waters by anglers.

Highland Park Distillery has a visitor centre just to the southeast of Kirkwall (on the A961 towards the Churchill Barriers). Their single malt whiskey is superb and has won many awards. Tel: (01856) 874619.

If you can manage to tear yourself away from all that sunken scrap metal, Orkney's Museums are a natural choice for anyone interested in the history of the islands. Of particular interest to those of us diving the sunken German Fleet are the Stromness Museum on Alfred Street,

Stromness and the Scapa Flow Visitor Centre and Museum at Lyness on the Island of Hoy. The Stromness Museum has a very fine collection of salvaged artifacts from the sunken German Fleet, including a couple of the German Ships' bells. The Museum at Lyness is generally visited at some point each week by the Orkney Dive Boats, as the centre is adjacent to a few excellent dive sites. The Museum and Visitor centre is housed in the original wartime buildings and tells the story of Scapa Flow's importance as a naval base since Napoleonic times. There is an impressive audio-visual display in an enormous old oil tank and the museum displays, though rather sad looking and run down for now, including hundreds of archive photographs are housed in the former pumping house. There is a good collection of military vehicles and several salvaged guns, as well as one of *HMS Hampshire's* propellers. The Naval Cemetery is located just a short walk away and has many of those lost in both wars including those from *HMS Royal Oak*. You can also reach the Museum by catching the regular ferry from Houton to Lyness on Hoy.

Orkney Heritage, Tel: (01856) 873191; www.orkneyheritage.com

There is another museum also worth spending some time in and that is the Orkney Wireless Museum, located at Kiln Corner, Junction Road in Kirkwall. It is essentially a local collection of memorabilia around old (and still working) radios. However there is an excellent display of wartime pictures and a display of the wartime radio equipment used in the defence of Scapa Flow. Contact details as above.

Founded in 1137, 22 years after St. Magnus was martyred, St.Magnus Cathedral is located on the main street of Kirkwall. It may be an unlikely tourist attraction, but the interior is superb, and the light from the stained glass windows diffuses throughout the building. There are many interesting Masonic tombs and a Memorial to the fallen from *HMS Royal Oak*.

The Neolithic Remains in Orkney achieved World Heritage status by UNESCO in 1999 and includes the superb Ring of Brodgar; the Standing Stones of Stenness; The tomb at Maeshowe; Barnhouse Village; the stone village of Skara Brae on the shore at Skaill and the Knowes of Trotty (where four remarkable gold discs were found). The Standing Stones around Orkney are particularly evident and no trip would be complete without seeing the Ring of Brodgar and the Standing Stones of Stenness. Both sites are exceptional, having been erected around 3500 BC (almost 1000 years before construction started on the Pyramids!).

The Kitchener Memorial at Marwick Head is very impressive. Erected after the loss of Lord Kitchener and *HMS Hampshire* in 1916, only 12 survivors out of 622 men, made it to shore. There was much controversy over the loss of the *Hampshire* and the almost total lack of rescuers; however the Memorial is still quite something. The walk from the small car park, where one of the salvaged guns from the Hampshire is displayed, is 1km long and takes you into the RSPB reserve on the cliffs.

Sea Stacks are common all around the shoreline and in particular the Old Man of Hoy (clearly evident as you approach and leave Orkney on the ferry) is superb. At 137m (450ft) high it was first climbed in 1966, it will take about a three hour round trip to walk to the site. Stanger Head on the Island of Flotta has two sea stacks called locally the Old Man and Woman of Flotta; the diving at Stanger Head around these low sea stacks is impressive. Yesnaby, just north of Inga Ness, along the western shore of Mainland is equally impressive. Here the almost relentless Atlantic surge has sculpted the shoreline into impressive caverns, caves, arches and sea stacks.

The Churchill Barriers are of course on everyone's list, as well as the Italian Chapel on Lamb Holm. The Barriers and Chapel were aided in construction by over 1350 Italian Prisoners of War conscripted by Winston Churchill, as a direct result of the loss of *HMS Royal Oak* to the German U-Boat *U-47*. These four barriers now connect South Ronaldsay, Burray, Glims Holm and Lamb Holm to Orkney Mainland. The erection of the Barriers has forever changed the ecology of the surrounding area and indeed, the effects of sand building up at Barrier 4 between Burray and South Ronaldsay have all but obliterated any reference to the ancient Blockships first placed in the water as protection to Scapa Flow. You can of course shore dive the blockships at the other three barriers, all are excellent shallow dives and a pleasant change from the much deeper German Fleet. To reach the Barriers and the Italian Chapel, take the A961 from Kirkwall south towards South Ronaldsay.

There are two Martello Towers on either side of Longhope Bay on the Island of Hoy. Built in 1813 to protect the Baltic convoys from the United States Navy and American privateers. The Hackness (south) tower is open to visitors and well worth seeing if you are already in the vicinity.

The Orkney wildlife also may not be on everyone's list, but many visitors each year make the pilgrimage to the islands to view the Common and Grey seals and of course the bird life. The RSPB has over 8000 hectares of reserves in Orkney and is involved in projects to care for Orkney's hen harrier and corncrake populations. The wetland meadows have red-throated divers, merganzers, otters and thousands of wildfowl. The sea cliffs and adjacent meadows in the late spring and early summer are thronged with over a million breeding seabirds including gannets, guillimots, shags, razorbills, kittiwakes, fulmars, puffins, gulls, terns and skuas. In the summer months minke whales, porpoises and orca are often seen by the ferry passengers travelling from Kirkwall to the outer islands, however porpoises only very occasionally venture into Scapa Flow. The rare Primula Scotica is found here and an amazing variety of other meadowland and wetland wild flowers can be found everywhere.

Orkney Jewellery is famous worldwide and a number of well known establishments are located around the islands and most gift shops have examples of the local designers work. Based largely on the historical Norse carvings, many exquisite pieces are there for your temptation! Ortak, Sheila Fleet and Aurora are three of the best known names.

There are a number of useful guidebooks available in the local shops, museums and visitor centres. Tel: (01856) 872856; www.visitorkney.com

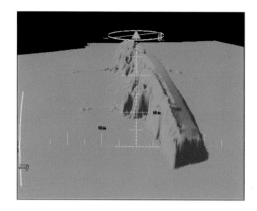

Sonar image of the Cöln II

The Scapa Map Project

ScapaMAP (Scapa Flow Marine Archeology Project) is a multi-disciplinary, multi-institution, international project involving government agencies, industry and the academic community, designed to document a unique marine archaeological area in the waters of Scapa Flow in the Orkney Islands of Scotland. In order to protect and monitor the wrecks for the future, ScapaMAP was initiated with the aim of constructing suitable base maps of the wrecks, recovery sites and other areas of interest in the Flow to aid in the interpretation, protection and monitoring of a significant local, national and international asset.

In early 2001, the ScapaMAP Acoustic Consortium (SAC) was formed with the aim of augmenting the project's other work with acoustic remote sensing data. The visibility of the water, its depth and temperature make it extremely difficult to carry out extensive diver measurement of the ships. Consequently, the only way to quickly map all of the wrecks and surrounding area to reasonable accuracy is to use an acoustic instrument.

Previous work has used sidescan sonar and shallow water multibeam equipment to provide medium resolution bathymetry and high resolution acoustic backscatter for the area. SAC chose to use a new, dynamically focused, very high resolution, multibeam echosounder (the Reson 8125) to provide the highest resolution data of the wreck and surrounding area to date.

The survey system provided by the SAC members consisted of the Reson 8125, a TSS POS/MV 320 attitude and navigation system, and a Racal Landstar DGPS receiver, installed aboard the S/V Scimitar.

The results from the sonar readings for the first time, quite clearly showed the exact state of each of the German Fleet, left on the seabed since 1919. The four remaining cruisers show a variety of states of decay. The *Cöln II* is probably the best preserved of the four, lying on its starboard side in about 35m of water. Careful inspection of the data shows the remaining portholes, superstructure, rear 6inch guns and even lifeboat davits to be in place. Extensive damage has been done to the rear hull in order to salvage the engine room non-ferrous materials, as with all of the remaining wrecks.

The *Brummer* and *Dresden II* have both suffered significant upper hull damage, the *Brummer's* forward plates collapsing, while the *Dresden's* weather-deck has fallen out to port, putting its forward guns into the sediment. Of all the wrecks, the *Karlsruhe II* is in poorest condition, principally due to extensive salvage work in the 1970's.

The three remaining battleships all turtled as they sank, mostly resting on the remaining superstructure, slowly crushing it with their own weight. The *Kronprinz Wilhelm* is mostly intact, except for the bow and engine room sections, while the *Markgraf* and *König* are in the poorest condition. Also in the area are the remains of the *Bayern*, at 28,000 tons the heaviest in the fleet. Prematurely over-pressured with compressed air during salvage attempts, the *Bayern* lifted off the ground too quickly, and left its four gun turrets behind before settling down, turned slightly towards the south east. Subsequent raising attempts were more successful, leaving behind only the turrets and some pieces of superstructure.

In addition to the industrial and academic partners involved directly, ScapaMAP received financial aid, or aid in kind, from the following sponsors: Historic Scotland; The Carnegie Fund for the Universities of Scotland; GSE Rentals Ltd., Aberdeen; TSS(UK)Ltd. and C-Map/USA.

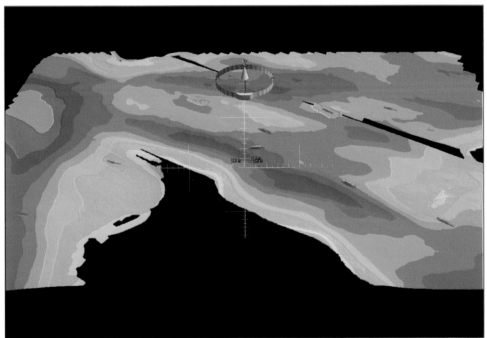

An overview of the Scapa Flow survey area depicting all of the remaining German fleet

An early German postcard showing the position of the Grand Fleet

Wrecks of the Grand Fleet

THE GERMAN BATTLESHIPS

Of the 74 ships comprising of 5 battle cruisers; 11 battleships; 8 light cruisers and 50 motor torpedo boat/destroyers from the German High Seas Battle Fleet that entered Scapa Flow under guard under a new ruling of internment on November 23rd 1918, virtually all of them would plunge beneath the waves a mere seven months later under direct orders of their Commander in Chief Ludwig von Reuter.

Over a period of 18 years, almost all of them were to be raised and salvaged in what is now regarded as the greatest feat of marine engineering and underwater salvage ever undertaken on the planet. The marine salvagers were so diligent in their task, that by 1945 and the end of the second world conflict they had only left behind three battleships to be visited by divers. These are the battleships *König, Kronprinz Wilhelm* and the *Markgraf*. The salvagers were a rather untidy lot and they also left four major debris sites: *Bayern , Seydlitz, Kaiser* and the *von der Tann.*

The author and publishers have deliberately excluded the GPS coordinates from all of the wreck sites to aid in their protection, as there are still unscrupulous divers who try and remove historic artifacts. These ships are all protected under the Protection of Wrecks Acts, 1973 and must not be tampered with in any way. Those independent divers wishing to visit Orkney and dive in Scapa Flow are advised to first get in touch with members of the Orkney Dive Boat Operators Association (OBDOA) www.obdoa.co.uk

Left: An overview of the Scapa Flow survey area depicting all of the Remaining German Fleet

BATTLECRUISERS

Derfflinger (The Derfflinger was used briefly as a blockship whilst waiting for the chosen hulks to arrive and be sunk).	Raised by Metal Industries	1939
Hindenburg	Raised by Cox and Danks	1930
Moltke	Raised by Cox and Danks	1927
Seydlitz	Raised by Cox and Danks	1928
Von der Tann	Raised by Cox and Danks	1930

BATTLESHIPS

Baden (Used for naval gunnery practice and sunk off Portsmouth in 1921)	Beached and saved	
Bayern	Raised by Metal Industries	1933
Frederich der Grosse (Her bell is on display in Stromness Museum)	Raised by Metal Industries	1937
Grosser Kurfürst	Raised by Metal Industries	1938
Kaiser	Raised by Cox and Danks	1929
Kaiserin	Raised by Metal Industries	1936
König	Salvage abandoned, still at Scapa Flow.	
König Albert	Raised by Metal Industries	1935
Kronprinz Wilhelm	Salvage abandoned, still at Scapa Flow.	
Prinzregent Luitpold	Raised by Cox and Danks	1931
Markgraf	Salvage abandoned, still at Scapa Flow.	

*A wonderful old photograph shows the whaler Ramna high and dry on the Moltke's hull,
after she ran aground on her on 23rd June 1919.*

The scuttled Hindenburg at rest on the seabed

KÖNIG

(X) **Location:**   West of Cava

(•) **Depth:**   18-42m (60-136ft)

(•) **Conditions:** Deep, dark and dismal!

(!) **Special Considerations:**

The only interesting parts are actually underneath the ship and only those divers qualified in penetration techniques should consider entering the zone.

(→) **Access:**   By boat only.

(•) **Diver Experience:**

Experienced in deep wreck diving recommended.

The *König, Kronprinz Wilhelm* and *Markgraf* are all *König* Class Battleships. The *König* was built by Kaiserliches Werft at Wilhelmshaven and was launched on 1st March 1913 displacing over 25,000 tons. All three ships are 174m (575ft) long, with a beam of 27m (97ft) and a draught of 9m (30ft). She was powered by three coal and oil fired engines which could push her through the water at 23knots. The *König* had been the flagship of the Third Battle Squadron during the Battle of Jutland and received ten direct hits! She finally sank at 14.00 hours on 21st June 1917.

Sadly Nundy (Marine Metals) Ltd blew her hull apart in the 1960's and 1970's in the quest for non-ferrous scrap and now the ship is in a terrible state of deterioration. All of her guns are hidden from view, trapped underneath the ship when she turned turtle, much of the stern and bows are intact, but the mid section is just a mess of gaping black holes amidst twisted metal. To my rather jaded (photographic) eyes, the only thing of interest on the dive is the great amount of marine growth on the flatter sections of the upturned hull with plumose anemones; brittle starfish; feather starfish; nudibranchs; shrimps; crabs and a huge variety of fish.

The König's upturned hull is covered in a mass of marine life

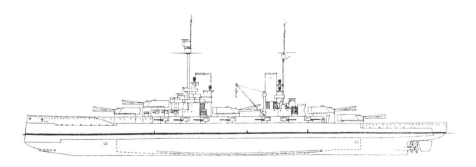

KRONPRINZ WILHELM

⊗ **Location:** West of Cava and north of the König.

☻ **Depth:** 12-38m (40-156ft)

✋ **Conditions:** Better light than on the other Battleships, but can still be very dark, with poor visibility.

❗ **Special Considerations:**

This is the shallowest of the Battleships, but also the worst for wear and great care should be taken when passing over the hull to the seabed before you start exploring the ship's more recognizable parts.

➔ **Access:** By boat only.

☋ **Diver Experience:**

Intermediate to Advanced with some wreck training recommended.

The *Kronprinz Wilhelm* was the last of the *König* Class battleships to be built and was built at Krupps Germania shipyard at Kiel and was launched on 21st February 1914. Almost identical to the *König* and *Markgraf*, they carried ten 12-inch guns and fourteen 5.9-inch guns, numerous antiaircraft guns and five submerged torpedo tubes. She came through the Battle of Jutland unscathed but did receive a torpedo hit by the British submarine J1 in November 1916. Fully repaired she languished with all of the other German Fleet until she travelled up to Scapa Flow and sank with her sister ships on 21st June 1919.

The *Kronprinz Wilhelm's* stern and bows are fairly intact and her upside down angle is less severe than that of the *König*. Her two rudders still stand proud of the ship and although the entire midships of the hull are a shambles, the underside of her port side is well worth exploring. Both masts and spotting top are splayed out on the muddy seabed, which is absolutely littered with jumbled bits of wreckage and mussel shell debris. Gun turrets are visible as are quite a number of empty portholes, but it is difficult to recognize and understand her present layout without many dives. The marine life is excellent and her hull is covered in dead men's fingers; plumose anemones; starfish; sea urchins; shrimps and crabs, I even found an angler fish on the hull, much more interesting. Saying that, and still accounting for her massive deterioration, the *Kronprinz Wilhelm* is a worthy dive and you should enjoy her secrets.

The Kronprinz Wilhelm photographed just before she was scuttled

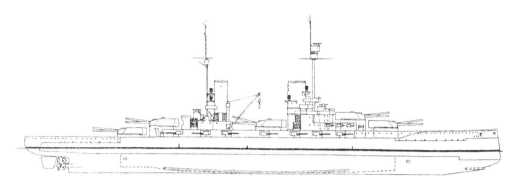

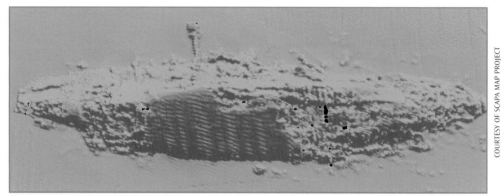

COURTESY OF SCAPA MAP PROJECT

The barrel of the large aft gun of the Kronprinz Wilhelm

MARKGRAF

(X) **Location:** Midway between the König and the Kronprinz Wilhelm.

(⌣) **Depth:** 25-44m (80-135ft)

(⌣) **Conditions:** Very similar to the other two battleships.

(!) **Special Considerations:**
Be careful when travelling down holding on to the positioning buoys as lion's mane jellyfish tentacles get wrapped up in them during the summer months, so also be careful when coming back up to the surface as you may just come upon one of these stinging giants.

(→) **Access:** By boat only.

(⌣) **Diver Experience:**
Advanced diver with wreck skills is recommended.

The *Markgraf* is almost identical to the *König* and the *Kronprinz Wilhelm* and was built by A.G.Weser at Bremen. She was launched on 4th June 1913 and formed part of the Third Battle Squadron and required over 1100 men to keep her at battle stations. She received quite a number of hits during the Battle of Jutland, but lived to survive another day, where Mother Fate would still be waiting for her. As she started to sink that afternoon of June 1919, she was boarded by a Royal Marine boarding party; sadly during a skirmish on board, the German captain Lt-Cdr Walther Schumann was killed. His grave can be found at Lyness Naval Cemetery.

The *Markgraf* now rests on her port side with her starboard underside still exposed. There is only about 4m (13ft) of space between the edge of the deck and the seabed and much of that is filled with debris. However, many divers absolutely love this dive as you can see the main gun turrets amidships and several of her smaller armaments. Portholes and dark holes beacon the unwary diver and the foremast and spotting top are now stretched out across the seabed. Her anchor chain hawse and anchor chain are also clearly visible. Although her stern is relatively intact, there are massive gaping wounds just before it, but both of her rudders still stand at least three metres (10ft) high, unmistakable.

The Markgraf at rest in Scapa Flow

A British naval party get ready to board one of the sinking German Fleet

The Kaiser Main Mast top lies in 22m (73ft)

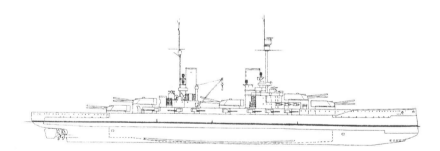

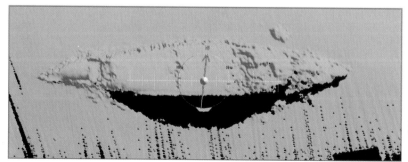

COURTESY OF SCAPA MAP PROJECT

Right: The exposed superstructure of the Battleships is covered in plumose anemones

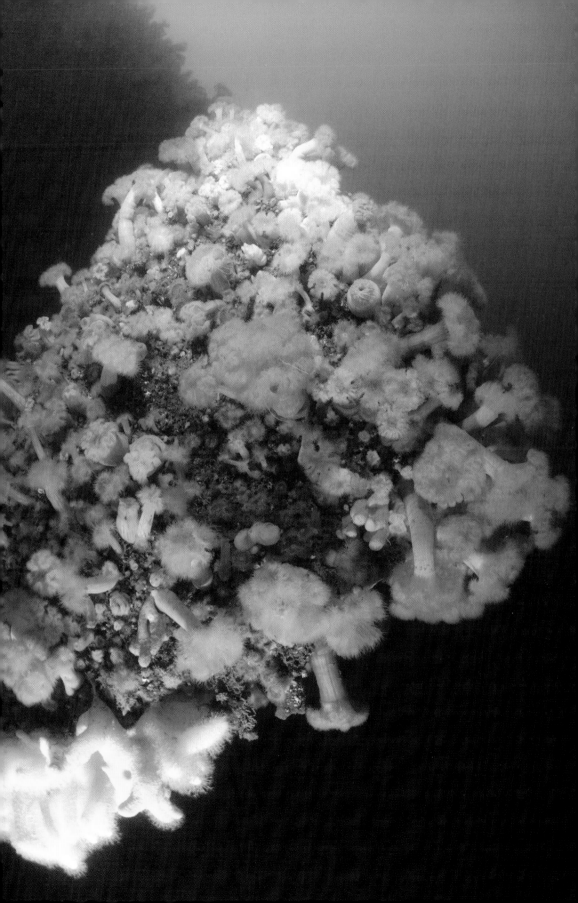

KAISER DEBRIS SITE

Location: Midway between the Karlsruhe II and the S36.

Depth: 22m (73ft)

Conditions: Some current is to be expected.

Special Considerations: Initial debris field is quite small, but other large sections are nearby, including a former work barge.

Access: By boat only.

Diver Experience: Suitable for all levels of diver.

The *Kaiser* was raised and salvaged by Cox and Danks in 1929 and in a similar situation to that of the other battleships, whatever was in the way, they just cut off, removed and left the bits on the seabed. In the initial pile there are two main mast sections, several smaller mast parts, spotting top, derrick hawsers, winch mechanisms, one huge block and tackle over 2 metres (6.5ft) high and several smaller blocks and tackle, standing rigging, clamps and many smaller assorted bit of unidentifiable German battleship. Both of the larger mast tops have pulley wheels in place. All of the metal parts are covered in a patina of purple encrusting algae and being so deep, have little kelp or other algae growth. Common sea urchins can be found on the parts.

The seabed is made up of fine sand and silt with several exposed rocky outcrops. There are queen scallops, scallops, burrowing starfish, burrowing anemones, turret shells, cuckoo wrasse, ballan wrasse, dog whelks and other molluscs.

Kaiser Hawser Pulley

VON DER TANN DEBRIS SITE

⊗ **Location:** Off the eastern-most headland of Rysa Little

☺ **Depth:** 15m – 18m(50 - 60ft)

✋ **Conditions:** Some current is to be expected.

❗ **Special Considerations:**
Debris field is large and spread out with many other parts from other ship salvage within the vicinity.

➔ **Access:** By boat only.

🤿 **Diver Experience:**
Suitable for all levels of diver.

The *von der Tann* was raised by Cox & Danks in 1930 and pulled over this sloping rocky headland, as they did with a number of other salvaged ships. The depth of the rocky reef off the headland was the same depth of the water at the Rosyth breaking yards, so any submerged parts that stuck on the rocks, Cox and Danks just blasted them off and left the bits where they were! There is loads of wreckage in this area including several guns, masts, spotting tops, the remains of two small pinnaces and an aeroplane's engine block (possibly matches with the parts at Lyness Museum on Hoy).

There is a huge amount of wreckage in this area, encrusted in colourful algae and sea urchins"

Buddy George Hendry on the Seydlitz anchor

BAYERN DEBRIS SITES (THE GUN TURRETS)

⊗ Location: The most easterly of all the battleship sites.

👁 Depth: 25-36m (80-120ft)

👁 Conditions: Generally poor visibility on the muddy seabed.

⚠ Special Considerations:
There is very little else to see here and it is certainly not worth the swim to the other pair of, now crushed' gun turrets.

➔ Access: By boat only.

⏱ Diver Experience:
Intermediate to advanced is recommended.

Whilst only a short dive, principally due to the depth and time constraints due to other deep dives in the vicinity, the *Bayern* gun turrets are quite interesting. During the salvage of the 28,000 ton *Bayern* by Metal Industries in 1934, they experienced a problem when one of the compressor hoses broke inside the hull. When the *Bayern* had sunk in 1919, she turned turtle

and her superstructure and guns sank deep into this softer area of Scapa Flow's seabed. After 14 years on the bottom, it was decided to pump her full of air to try and get her clear of the cloying mud.

The upturned ball race from the Bayern's aft guns

Suddenly the *Bayern* wrenched herself free from the bottom and launched herself through the surface leaving her four sets of massive guns and turrets. Her gun turrets were not

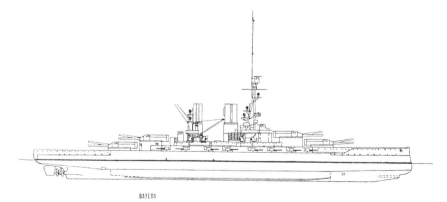

BAYERN

Line drawing of the battleship Bayern

locked in place, rather they were held in by their weight alone and were able to be turned using a massive ballrace. Located to the north east of the *Kronprinz Wilhelm,* the compressed air suddenly burst from the ship and the *Bayern* sunk once more, but at a different angle. She plowed down and crushed her

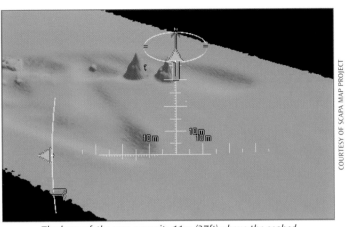

COURTESY OF SCAPA MAP PROJECT

The base of the gun now sits 11m (37ft) above the seabed

forward guns into the mud, but missed her aft gun turrets completely. She was subsequently raised again without further incident, but her main gun turrets are still on the seabed.

Visibility was around 2m (6.5ft) when I visited the site in the summer of 2005. The tops (or rather the underside) of the turrets stand almost 11m (36ft) above the seabed now littered with marine shell debris. The sides of the turret are open and for those foolhardy enough, you could possibly get inside them

(Hah!) anyway, the gun barrels are not visible and the main part of the turret now actually extends underneath the seabed. What is interesting, is the massive ballrace of the turret, still in place. The huge steel ball-bearings look like a row of canon balls. The entire area was surrounded by schools of fish and the sloping muddy seabed was home to all manner of interesting marine critters. Not a lot of dive for a lot of effort, but interesting nonetheless.

The battleship Bayern sinking

SEYDLITZ DEBRIS SITE

⊗ **Location:** Southwest from the Point of the Ward at Cava.

◎ **Depth:** 15-21m (50-70ft)

◎ **Conditions:** Some current is to be expected.

⚠ **Special Considerations:**
None really, as this is a great dive!

➔ **Access:** By boat only.

◔ **Diver Experience:**
Suitable for all levels of diver.

The *Seydlitz* was raised by Cox and Danks back in 1928, but they were a rather untidy lot then and left lots of interesting bits behind, particularly one of her massive guns! This now sits partly hidden in the soft shell and gravel seabed, but the barrel still points upwards. There are large sections of the mast, searchlights and other interesting German ship parts. This site is in an area of clean sand, with small silty parts where low algae grows. There is little sedimentation and small outcroppings of bedrock can be found, one outcrop is underneath one of the Seydlitz's anchors giving it the visual effect of almost floating above the seabed. Nearby can be found two massive salver's concrete Blocks, one with a huge eye on it, the other with railway track protrusions. The barge used in this salvage is also located nearby.

One small gun lies partly buried in the sand, whilst another is partly hidden underneath her shielding and the more obvious gun is one part of an anti-ship cannon, one of a pair, which now sits almost upright from her shielding. A huge spotting top sits in the middle of this area and you can see steel hawsers wrapped around her, obviously used as an anchor during the salvage of the Seydlitz

The Seydlitz resting clear of Scapa waters on her starboard side

Right: One of four guns from the Seydlitz, dumped overboard during her salvage

Light Cruiser Bremse

German Light Cruisers

When the German High Seas Battle Fleet entered Scapa Flow on November 23rd 1918, there were also eight Light Cruisers included in the fleet for internment. As the entire fleet was scuttled under direct orders against the terms of the armistice, the Light Cruisers were some of the last to sink that day, seven months later. The *Bremse, Emden II, Frankfurt* and the *Nürnberg II* were all saved and beached by the Royal Navy, however the other four, comprising of the *Brummer, Cöln II, Dresden II* and the *Karlsruhe II* all plunged to the seabed and there they would remain.

The main reason why these light cruisers stayed underwater was that they were in a depth of water similar to the battleships and battlecruisers, but too small and light to waste precious time and equipment on their salvage, when the other monstrous battleships yielded so much money in scrap. Metal Industries and Nundy Marine Metals of course saw there worth after they had been abandoned by Cox & Danks and blasted their way into the ships' innards in the search for her precious non-ferrous metal.

The *Brummer, Cöln II* and *Dresden II* all belong to Okney Islands Council and for those independent divers wishing to visit these ships, permission to dive and a diving permit must be obtained from Orkney Islands Council Harbours Department at Scapa. The *Karlsruhe II* is privately owned by a salvage company who allow diving on her; but no salvage must take place, as all of the remaining German Fleet are now protected sites. Further information can be obtained from the Orkney Dive Boats Operators Association (OBDOA) . You will note the spelling of the *Cöln II*, as there have been other variations in the past. There was another *Köln*, but she was built and served in WWII. The recovered bell from the *Cöln II* is on display at the Lyness Visitor Centre on the Island of Hoy, where you can check out the correct spelling of the ship.

Left: An overview of Scapa Flow showing the positions of the German Light Cruisers
Previous page: Diver swimming along the deck of the Light Cruiser Cöln II

THE LIGHT CRUISERS

Bremse	Towed to shore and beached by *HMS Venetia* and the trawler *Clonsin*. Her cables unfortunately slipped and she capsized to starboard, just as she reached the shore. She was salvaged by Cox & Danks in 1929. There was some local controversy over the identity of this ship, as a local family extensively liberated some of her non-ferrous metal parts left behind after Cox & Danks slipshod salvage. The only name identification that they could find on her engine parts was Frankfurt, raising local speculation as to which ship was actually salvaged and which ship was sent to the United States. However it would appear that the *Bremse* was a Frankfurt Class Light Cruiser. One of her salvaged guns is on display at Lyness Visitor Centre.
Brummer	Salvage abandoned, still at Scapa Flow.
Cöln II	Salvage abandoned, still at Scapa Flow.
Emden II	Saved by *HMS Shakespeare* and was not sunk. She was later handed over to France in 1920 and was finally scrapped in 1926
Dresden II	Salvage abandoned, still at Scapa Flow. An interesting note discovered in the National Archives had the *Dresden II* salvaged and sent to the United States raising doubts as to the identity of the fourth Light Cruiser still on the seabed. However the *Dresden* was the only Light Cruiser that had an identifying shield at her bows and this is still clearly visible today.
Frankfurt	Towed to shore and beached by *HMS Wessex* and subsequently refloated by the Royal Navy. Sold to the United States, where she was used for aerial bombing experiments and was sunk off Cape Henry on 18th July 1921.
Karlsruhe II	Salvage abandoned, still at Scapa Flow.
Nürnberg II	Beached by *HMS Walpole* and the Trawler *Clonsin* and retained by the British Admiralty. It was later used as gunnery practice by the British Navy and finally sunk between Portsmouth and the Isle of Wight on 7th February, 1922..

BREMSE (SITE ONLY)

⊗ **Location:** Just around the corner from the pier at Swanbister Bay and west of Orphir Bay, at Toy Ness. Some anchor chain and cables can be identified on the shore.

⊙ **Depth:** 3-18m (10-60ft).

◉ **Conditions:** Little to no current and very sheltered from northerly winds.

⚠ **Special Considerations:**
Shore access is a bit of a trek and it is recommended to do this from a boat for ease of comfort.

➔ **Access:** Access can be gained through the local farmer's field, but permission must be gained first and always close any farm gates behind you.

◔ **Diver Experience:**
Beginner

Salvaged gun from the Bremse

The *Bremse* was built by A.G. Vulcan at Stettin, along with her sister ship the *Brummer* and was 139m (456ft) long, weighing 4,308 tons. When the *Bremse* was run aground by *HMS Venetia* and the trawler *Clonsin,* she heeled over to starboard and her forward gun turret fell off her. Unwanted by the salvage company, this was largely ignored when Cox and Danks broke the ship apart in 1929. Cox and Danks were a rather untidy lot and they left many odd bits of metal including two masts, bollards, various pipes, engine parts, the gun race, steering gears and quite a number of hull plates. Interestingly, although the ship first capsized to starboard, much of her hull remains are listing to port. The shallower sections are well covered in kelp and other seaweeds, which in turn are grazed upon by various wrasse species and sea urchins. Her forward gun was salvaged and is now on display at the Lyness Visitor Centre on the Island of Hoy.

Cox & Danks raise an upturned Destroyer.

BRUMMER

Location: Lying in a northwesterly direction between the Kronprinz Wilhelm and the Cöln II.

Depth: 24-36m (77-120ft).

Conditions: Little current to speak of, but can be quite dark on the morning dives.

Special Considerations:
There is heavy deterioration at the bows of the ship and huge sections are coming apart, it is recommended to keep your distance from this area when examining it.

Access: By boat only.

Diver Experience:
Beginner to Intermediate, but should have some wreck diving experience.

The *Brummer* was built by A.G. Vulcan at Stettin and was also a *Bremse* Class Light Cruiser. She was originally designed and built in 1913 and was launched on 11th December 1915. Built for speed in mine-laying activities, she weighed 4,308 tons and was 139m (456ft) long. Only armed with four 150mm (5.9inch) guns mounted along the ship's centre line, she also had two 85mm (3.4inch) anti-aircraft guns mounted behind the last of her three funnels. She was capable of carrying 360 mines and her twin turbine engines, working in tandem could push her along at an incredible thirty-four knots. The *Brummer* sank beneath the waves at 13.05 on 21st June 1919.

Extremely popular with divers, the *Brummer* rests on her starboard side and lies in a northwesterly direction. As you descend down the shotline to the edge of her deck, her most distinctive feature is the railings on top of her bridge. This former viewing platform is not present on any other ship in Scapa Flow and is covered in seasquirts, dead men's fingers and feather starfish. Forward from this is the armoured command centre with its horizontal viewing slits and gun control range finder (this looks a bit like a modern radar in shape – but radar wasn't in place until the Second World War). Forward from the bridge can be found a shielded 150mm, 45calibre (5.9inch) deck gun on a pedestal mount. Sadly the distinctive bows are deteriorating rapidly and the decks are coming away from the ship's hull, but are still impressive nonetheless. Now that this section is opening up, more access can be gained into the interior, for those who wish to do so!

One of the other distinctive factors in exploring the *Brummer*, is that the seabed is relatively clean of wreckage debris but there are tons of mollusc shell debris where long clawed squat lobsters *(Munida rugosa)* can be found. Her stern is largely intact and entry can be made into the officers' accommodation and of course, her stern guns are always worth visiting. Many divers comment on still finding iron portholes, still with glass in them, always a delight!

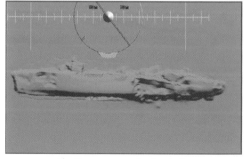

The Brummer as she lies today

CÖLN II

Location:
East of the Brummer, due north of the Dresden II and northwest from the Barrel of Butter.

Depth:
18-36m (60-120ft).

Conditions:
Generally a bit murky at the bottom, due to the silty nature of the site.

Special Considerations:
Beware of lion's mane jellyfish tentacles trapped on the shot line to the wreck, as they can sweep across your face or hands, leaving a dreadful sting.

Access:
By boat only.

Diver Experience:
Intermediate to advanced with some wreck diving experience essential.

One of the *Dresden II* Class of cruisers, the *Cöln II* was built at the Blohm and Voss Shipyards in Hamburg and was 155.5m (510ft) long and weighed 5,620 tons. She was officially classed by the German Navy as a small protected cruiser and was armed with eight 150mm (5.9inch) guns, two 50 calibre anti aircraft guns and even had four torpedo tubes, two of which were underwater and the other two situated on either side of the deck just forward of the middle funnel.

The most intact of all the High Seas Battle Fleet, now resting on her starboard side, descending divers tend to land near the bridge area, davits and forward mast that stretches off to the seabed and still has her crow's nest intact. One of the most distinctive views is of one of her guns with her shielding gone, now silhouetted against the skyline. There are still plenty of (iron) portholes and many openings lead to the officers' accommodation and other areas of the ship. The midsection of the hull is quite damaged and large gaping holes open up beneath you, but most divers drop down to the seabed and swim along to either the bows or the stern.

Many divers rate this extremely high for penetration, but most visitors are quite content to amble along the now vertical deck and spend time viewing the various gun emplacements and other more recognisable bits.

The Cöln II remains remarkably intact

DRESDEN II

(X) **Location:** The most southerly located of the Light Cruisers and Battleships, the Dresden II lies midway between the Barrel of Butter and Cava.

(☺) **Depth:** 16-38m (53-125ft).

(☺) **Conditions:** Visibility is generally better in the southern area of Scapa Flow as the tidal stream pushes past here and the slight current keeps her relatively clean.

(!) **Special Considerations:**
There is still a lot of silt on the ship and diving too close to the hull will inevitably spoil the dive for those following you.

(→) **Access:** By boat only.

(☺) **Diver Experience:**
Beginner to Intermediate, with some wreck experience recommended.

The *Dresden II* was built at Howaldtswerke Dockyards in Kiel, Germany and launched in April 1917. The signature design of the *Dresden II* Class of Light Cruiser, she was identical in design and size as her sister ship the *Cöln II*, but had a slightly different configuration in her gun positions, with her main armaments placed on the lower deck, either side of the bridge. She weighed 5,531 tons and was 153m (502ft) long, capable of launching 200 mines from her stern she saw regular service in the North Sea until she was holed by a torpedo from a British submarine. She was still undergoing repairs at Stettin when news of the internment was posted. She joined the rest of the High Seas Fleet only to be scuttled and finally sank at 13.30 hours.

Fairly intact, the *Dresden II* lies on her port side, facing west of north with her bows, bridge and stern perhaps the most interesting aspects of the ship. Her bows are in 30m (100ft) and the seabed slopes off to the stern at around 38m (125ft). The shallowest part of the wreck is above the bridge section, where it is only 16m (52.5ft), the shelter deck and her main mast combined with the armoured lookout post lies out from the ship and stretches to the seabed. Much of the forward deck is starting to peel away from the hull and therefore much of this area is in the shade as the deck now leans over so far, undoubtedly it will completely detach itself from the hull and this will start even further deterioration. One of her anchor chains runs out from the starboard anchor hawse and terminates some 50m (165ft) away at a rather large and impressive anchor. Very slender in style, her bows are still in good shape and makes for a superb photographic backdrop and on the top of the starboard side just behind the bows can be found her identifying shield, quite clearly defined. The ship's stern is perhaps the most interesting with her two 10mm (5.9inch) guns, one of which is still attached, with the other now lying on the seabed.

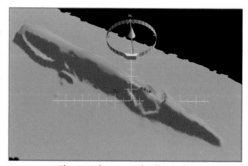

The Dresden II as she lies today

KARLSRUHE II

⊗ **Location:** Northwest of the northwesterly tip of Cava.

⊙ **Depth:** 14-27m (46-89ft).

◍ **Conditions:** Visibility is generally poor in this silty region, but being shallower than the other wrecks, there is more ambient light.

! **Special Considerations:**

The Karlsruhe II has the worst deterioration of all the German Fleet and care should be taken over entanglement of equipment.

→ **Access:** By boat only.

☺ **Diver Experience:**

Beginner to Intermediate, but some wreck diving experience is recommended.

The Karlsruhe II at sea

The *Karlsruhe II* is the worst deteriorated of all the German Fleet, but still ranks very highly on all Scapa Flow divers' list, due to her shallow depth. Often used as a 'warm-up' dive before tackling the deeper wrecks, invariably divers will come back and do it a second time, because it was so much fun the first!

Built at Kaiserliche Werft Shipyards at Willhelmshaven she was 150.8m (495ft) long and weighed 5,440 tons at her launch on 31st January 1916. One of four *Konigsberg (ii)* class of Light cruisers, her high-pressure navy turbines were powered by twelve boilers, ten coal and two oil fired. Her armament included eight 150mm (5.9inch) guns, three 85mm (3.45inch) guns, four batteries of 50mm anti aircraft guns, and was capable of handling 120 mines.

The shallowest of all the Light Cruisers, it is only 25m (80ft) to the seabed near the stern of the *Karlsruhe II*, which is now also lying on her starboard side. She is well broken up and her stern has sunk considerably into the soft mud and shelly sea floor. However the sheer scale of the ship is still incredibly impressive. Her guns are also slowly sinking into the seabed and even the distinctive anchor that used to hang high up on her stern is gradually sinking into the silt. Huge iron portholes still stud the hull and open companionways invite you further into the ship's interior. Access into her interior is relatively easy for those properly qualified, but the general rule is to stay on the outside of the ship due to the massive deterioration that is overtaking these once proud naval ships.

Most of railings, davits, masts and other more exposed sections are covered in plumose anemones; feather starfish; seasquirts; brittle starfish and various species of crabs, shrimps and nudibranchs. Her bow guns are still impressive as is the anchor windlass and chain and whilst this wreck is in the worst condition, it is possibly the most popular as there is so much more ambient light and of course much more time to explore her shallow aspect.

The Cöln II is one of the most popular of the Light Cruisers

MAINLAND

Bremse Site

Orphir Bay

Bayern Turret Site

Brummer

Cöln II

Kronprinz Wilhelm

Karlsruhe II

Markgraf

Barrel of Butter

Kaiser Site

König

Dresden II

S36

CAVA

Coal Barge

Seydlitz Site

V83

Von Der Tann Site

V78

Vanguard

RYSA LITTLE

Gutter
Sound

West
Weddell Sound

Prudentia

Concrete
Barge

Reef Dive

YC21

F2

Nevi
Skerry

B109

FARA

Mara

UB116

Steam Pinner
Stern Section

HMS Strathgarry

Rose
Valley

FLOTTA

S54

Hoxa
Head

HOY

Roedean

Stanger
Head

Kirk Bay

James Barrie

SWITHA

SOUTH WALLS

| 1 | 0 | 1 | 2 | 3 | 4 Kilometres |

Scale

MTB Destroyers beached in Scapa Flow

Motor Torpedo Boats (Destroyers)

The remaining compliment of the German High Seas Battle Fleet that were anchored between Hoy and Cava around the Gutter Sound area included what was originally accounted for as forty-four destroyer/torpedo boats, was in fact fifty ships from five flotillas. Five of the Torpedo boats are still diveable and one of the ships, previously designated only as the 'MTB', has been positively identified by Kevin Heath as the *V 78*. The original admiralty chart of the ship's positions was written in rough script and what looked like MTB was actually *V78*. Further proof came from the recovered telegraph that has now been returned to her homeport of Stettin in Germany.

German Destroyers and Large Torpedo Boats were basically the same and had very little distinction between them. The term Destroyer did not come into effect with the German Navy until the B.97 class that was built in 1914/1915. Until this time the Torpedo Boats and Destroyers were not named, rather they were identified with a consecutive number and a letter denoting the Naval yard it was built at.

B = Blohm & Voss Shipyards in Hamburg.

G = Germania-Werft A.G. at Kiel.

H = Howaldtswerke Dockyards in Kiel.

S = Schichau-Werft Shipyard at Elbing.

V = A. C. Vulcan Shipyard at Stettin.

First Flotilla:
G 38; G 39; G 40; G 86; S 32; V 129.

Second Flotilla:
B 109; B 110; B 111; B 112; G 101; G 102; G 103; G104; S 138; V 100.

Third Flotilla:
S 53; S 54; S 55; G 91; V 70; V 73; V 81; V 82.

Sixth Flotilla:
S 49; S 50; S 131; S 132; V 43; V 44; V 45; V 46; V 125; V 126; V127; V 128.

Seventh Flotilla:
H 145; G 89; G 92; S 36; S 51; S 52; S 56; S 60; S 65; S 136; S 137; S 138; V 78; V83.

Ship	Sunk/Beached	Fate
B 109	Sunk	Salvaged, March 1926
B 110	Sunk	Salvaged, December 1925
B 111	Sunk	Salvaged, March 1926
B 112	Sunk	Salvaged, February 1926
G 38	Sunk	Salvaged, September 1924
G 39	Sunk	Salvaged, July 1925
G 40	Sunk	Salvaged, July 1929
G 86	Sunk	Salvaged, 1923
G 89	Sunk	Salvaged, December 1922
G 91	Sunk	Salvaged, September 1924
G 92	Beached	Retained by Admiralty, scrapped in 1922
G 101	Sunk	Salvaged, April 1926
G 102	Beached	Sent to USA, sunk as target 1921
G 103	Sunk	Raised and salvaged, sunk in storm 1925
G 104	Sunk	Raised and salvaged, scrapped April 1926
H 145	Sunk	Salvaged, March 1925
S 32	Sunk	Salvaged, June 1925
S 36	Sunk	Salvaged, April 1925
S 49	Sunk	Salvaged, December 1924
S 50	Sunk	Salvaged, October 1924
S 51	Beached	Retained by Admiralty, scrapped in 1922
S 52	Sunk	Salvaged, October 1924
S 53	Sunk	Salvaged, June 1924
S 54	Sunk	Salvaged, September 1921
S 55	Sunk	Salvaged, August 1924
S 56	Sunk	Salvaged, June 1925
S 60	Beached	Sent to Japan, scrapped in 1922
S 65	Sunk	Salvaged, May 1922
S 131	Sunk	Salvaged, August 1924
S 132	Beached	Sent to USA, sunk in 1921
S 136	Sunk	Salvaged, April 1925
S 137	Beached	Retained by Admiralty, scrapped in 1922
S 138	Sunk	Salvaged, May 1925

V 43	Beached	Sent to USA, sunk as target, 1921
V 44	Beached	Retained by Admiralty, scrapped in 1924
V 45	Sunk	Salvaged, 1922
V 46	Beached	Sent to France, scrapped in 1924
V 70	Sunk	Salvaged, August 1924
V 73	Beached	Retained by Admiralty, scrapped in 1922
V 78	Sunk	Salvaged, 1925
V 80	Beached	Sent to Japan, scrapped in 1922
V 81	Beached	Sunk on way to breakers yards, 1922
V 82	Beached	Retained by Admiralty, scrapped in 1922
V 83	Sunk	Scrapped in 1928
V 100	Beached	Sent to France, scrapped in 1921
V 125	Beached	Retained by Admiralty, scrapped in 1922
V 126	Beached	Sent to France, scrapped in 1925
V 127	Beached	Sent to Japan, scrapped in 1922
V 128	Beached	Retained by Admiralty, scrapped in 1922
V 129	Sunk	Salvaged and scrapped in 1922

The Destroyer/MTB's were the smallest of all the fleet and therefore easier to raise and scrap.

GERMAN FLEET 1919: MOTOR TORPEDO BOATS

B109

⊗ **Location:** North of Lyness Pier and close by the wrecks of the F2 and YC21.

😵 **Depth:** 10-12m (34-40ft)

🌀 **Conditions:** Slight current and a fairly clean sandy bottom, covered in shell debris.

⚠ **Special Considerations:**
Fairly easy dive, better for the marine life photography than wreck-spotting.

➔ **Access:** By boat only.

😑 **Diver Experience:**
Suitable for all levels of diver.

The *B109* was a small German Torpedo Boat and part of the 4th Division, No.2 Flotilla and one of a large group which all sunk together in Gutter Sound. Refloated and gutted, she was first used as a working platform to aid the salvage of the larger battleships. She was eventually scrapped with her bows and stern removed and the rest unceremoniously dumped back in Gutter Sound. She was first identified as the B109 in 1982 and her remains lie on their port side. There is no recognizable superstructure and what is there is about 14m (46ft) long and shaped like an irregular box. The top is fringed in seaweeds and there is plenty of marine life on and around her.

Hermit crabs are very common on the kelp covering of this wreck

MTB (Destroyers) at anchor in Scapa Flow

S36

(X) **Location:** Off the western shore of Cava, north of Taing Head.

(⌾) **Depth:** 5-11m (17-37ft)

(⌾) **Conditions:** Very little current, certainly nothing to bother the dive!

(!) **Special Considerations:**

The seabed is very muddy and the visibility is generally reduced in this area of Rysa Sound.

(→) **Access:** By boat only.

(⌾) **Diver Experience:**

Suitable for all levels of diver.

The S36 was originally part of the 17th Division of No.7 Flotilla, built at the Schichau yard at Elbing. After her seacocks had been pulled, she was luckily driven ashore by the Navy. She was refloated by Cox and Danks in 1925, gutted, run aground and beached on the western shore of Cava where huge steel hawsers were attached to her to keep the *Hindenburg* afloat during those salvage operations (and not the *V83* as originally thought). Once the *Hindenburg* was towed away, the S36 was scrapped where she lay. Her remains now litter the muddy seabed all the way into the rocky shoreline. Only part of her stern is identifiable, and the remains have a general ship's outline. There is no propeller and the drive shafts are still clearly visible amidst the other garbage and seaweeds. All of her bows and amidships are gone.

Surprisingly there is not as much kelp cover as on the other shallow wrecks, but there are plenty of fish as usual.

As the S36 is such a shallow wreck her remains are covered in seaweeds, dead men's fingers, sponges and plenty of interesting critters.

Dogfish are a common site around this wreckage

S54

(X) **Location:** Off the eastern coast of Flotta, midway between Lee Craig and Lentsy.

(🌀) **Depth:** 10-15m (33-50ft)

(🌀) **Conditions:** Quite a sheltered bay with no current.

(!) **Special Considerations:**
Watch out for seals here, but they are rather skittish.

(→) **Access:** By boat only.

(🌀) **Diver Experience:**
Suitable for all levels of diver.

S 53 – 66 (191S)

The S54 was part of No.3 Flotilla, also built at the Schichau yard at Elbing and sustained little damage when she was first scuttled. She had been refloated by Cox & Danks and was being towed south when the weather worsened and she broke her tow ropes and drifted ashore south of Lee Craig. The boulder slope here quickly made short work of her and she sank. The vessel was salvaged a second time, but the salvagers did this in-situ and literally blew her apart. There is very little left of the wreck and all of this is on the clean sandy bottom. The boulder slope is covered in kelp and there are lots of gullies with squat lobsters; blennies and gobies. Part of the deck house lies to the north adjacent to shore, but the main section visible is the turbines and heat exchangers. Lying roughly in a north to south direction, the bay abounds with seals and should your interest wane in the wreck, the seals will keep you entertained.

Heat Exchanger

Engine parts

Engine parts

V78

(X) **Location:** Off North Point on the Island of Fara.

(~) **Depth:** 8-10m (27-33ft)

(~) **Conditions:** Slight current running around the corner; site can be exposed to north easterly winds.

(!) **Special Considerations:**

Area is a bit silty, so try not to stir up the sediment too much; there are also lots of jagged bits of metal around, which could snag an expensive suit.

(→) **Access:** By boat only.

(~) **Diver Experience:**

Suitable for all levels of diver.

V 67 – 84 (1917)

German MTB's/V78

Formerly referred to as the MTB, this wreck was positively identified by Kevin Heath, when he recovered her telegraph, which was quite clearly marked with the name. This telegraph was reported to the Receiver of Wreck and has eventually made its way back to Stettin, Germany where she had been originally built. The *V78* only looked like a torpedo boat and was in fact a destroyer; part of the 13th Division of No.7 Flotilla; the mistake in her identification was actually originally made by the Admiralty as the written numbers '78' on the chart looked similar to 'TB'. Whilst being towed to shore, to try and save her, she struck the boulder slope and capsized. There is very little of this salvaged vessel left, as much of her was raised by Cox and Danks in 1923, but her bridge section is still there, now upside down in the mud. Signal flags, two search lights and other bits of jumbled wreckage are still around, but most of the interesting bits have now been found.

The remains of the V78 are spread out over a wide area of the rocky slope

V83

⊗ **Location:** Off the eastern side or Risa Little near the small bay.

◉ **Depth:** 2-18m (6-60ft)

◉ **Conditions:** No current, but the seabed is a little silty

① **Special Considerations:**
Lots of jagged bits of metal about and lion's mane jellyfish tentacles can get caught on them, so do not touch if you are not wearing gloves, like I was!

→ **Access:** By boat only.

◉ **Diver Experience:**
Suitable for all levels of diver.

V 67 – 84 (1917)

The *V83*, like the others of her class was built by A.C.Vulcan at Stettin and joined the German Fleet in 1916. She was 81m (269ft) long and weighed 909 tons and was capable of 36knots. She was fitted with three guns and six forward mounted torpedo tubes and was capable of carrying 24 mines. The *V83* and the *G92* were beached on Rysa Little by the Royal Navy. The *G92* was refloated and towed away to be scrapped and the V83 was not used in the lifting operations of the *Hindenburg* as originally thought, she was scrapped where she lay. All of her forward section is gone, but her narrow stern is largely intact and access can be gained into the stern, with care of the plumose anemones. Both propshafts are visible; but there are no propellers. Plenty of edible crabs; octopus and various wrasse are generally found here. She lists slightly to port and the sides of the superstructure are now strewn over the seabed to starboard. Nearby can be found an old concrete barge which was probably used by Cox & Danks to scrap the *V83*.

G92 aground

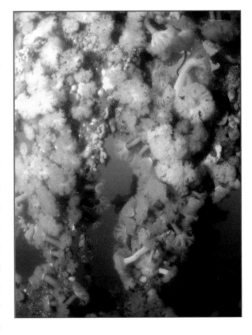

Interior view of the V83

Stern view of the V83

The V83 and G92 ashore off Rysa Little

COURTESY OF ORKNEY ARCHIVES

An aeroplane ditches in Scapa Flow

Aeroplane Wrecks in Scapa Flow

Whilst we are concentrating primarily on the many shipwrecks, the remains of which we are all enjoying today, there are also a number of aeroplane wrecks to be found. During World War II there were around 180 military aircraft either shot down or crash landed around the Orkney Islands. These included crash landings from aircraft carriers, losses due to adverse weather conditions, mid-air collisions, enemy aircraft shot down by the Anti-Aircraft Battery positions and forced landings due to engine troubles or some other such mechanical fault.

There is now documented evidence of at least eleven aircraft which have specifically crashed into the sea within the confines of Scapa Flow.

Date	Aircraft	Base/Squadron	Details
10/08/1917	Avenger	HMS Furious	Squadron Commander Dunning made the first ever landing and take-off from an aircraft carrier, on his second attempt to land, he crashed into the sea, over the starboard bow and was killed.
16/03/1940	Luftwaffe Aircraft	Luftwaffe	Crashed in sea, Scapa Flow
02/04/1940	JU88	Luftwaffe	Shot down by AA during a raid on Burray & Hoy, landed in sea. Crew lost.
08/04/1943	Defiant DR937	Twatt 771 Squadron	Hit barrage balloon cable in Scapa Flow, lost wingtip and crashed in sea. Crew saved.

Left: Diver swimming along the deck of the Light Cruiser Cöln II

20/04/1944	Barracuda II DP983	HMS Furious 830 Squadron	Struck Barrage Balloon cable and crashed into Scapa Flow. Crew unknown.
09/05/1944	Oxford I BG555	Skaebrae 598 Squadron	Crashed in Scapa Flow, east of Cava, on Army Co-operative Exercise. Three crew lost.
10/06/1944	Warwick I BV417	Wick281 Squadron	Ditched in Scapa Flow due to starboard engine failure. Crew recovered.
17/06/1944	Barracuda II BV922	HMS Furious 827 Squadron	Forced landing in Scapa Flow, due to supercharger or valve gear failure. Three crew picked up.
24/08/1944	Avenger Y155	HMS Trumpeter 846 Squadron	Crashed soon after take off from aircraft carrier and sank in 90 seconds. All four crew saved.
09/10/1944	JU88	Luftwaffe	Crashed in Scapa Flow, shot down by 611 Squadron from Skaebrae. Crew lost.
02/12/1944	Wildcat VI Mark VI JV751	HMS Trumpeter 846 Squadron	Crashed over port side of carrier in Scapa Flow. Crew saved.

We know from the Public Records Office that Metal Industries raised five lost aircraft as well as an additional two flying boats (possibly Catalinas - that are not in the official records), from within Scapa Flow, we also know of the location site of a further two aircraft, where parts have been recovered, one east of Cava and the other east of Rysa Little (Some of these parts are on display in the Lyness Museum). This still leaves four aircraft lost and unaccounted for within Scapa Flow.

The remains of the Irene beached on the shores of South Ronaldsay

Other Wrecks in Scapa Flow

Whilst Scapa Flow is synonymous with the German Battle Fleet, there are a number of other wrecks within and outside the flow. For this volume, the only ships discussed outside Scapa Flow are the loss of the *Hampshire* and the *Aorangi*, however many other shipwrecks are found around Orkney, all of which are superb and usually found in very clear water, a few are well worth a small mention at least.

Bella Vista	6,299 tons, lost off Papa Westray
Cotovia:	4,020 tons, lost south of Auskerry
Endeavour	Trawler lost at The String
Freesia	285 tons, lost at Eynhallow
Hastings County	4,178 tons, lost at Auskerry
Llama	3,189 tons, lost off Westray Sound
Manina	1,877 tons, lost off Sule Skerry
Monomoy	2,783 tons, lost off Marwick Bay
Loch Maddy	4,995 tons, lost at Inganess
Remus	1,079 tons, lost east of South Ronaldsay
St. Rognavald	486 tons, lost at Stronsay
Swiftsure	823 tons, lost off Shapinsay
Tennessee	5,667 tons, lost at Deerness
Tomalina	130ft Fish carrier, lost off Westray
Zarefah	279 tons, lost off Mull Head

Additional shipwrecks within the confines of Scapa Flow and directly related to the British Admiralty include the following small vessels which were used as armed patrols and boom defence craft.   Most have never been found, let alone dived!

Alberic	(ex Alberia) 286 ton steam trawler built by Cochrane & Sons of Selby and launched in 1910, sunk in collision 3rd May 1941
Catherine	Drifter built in 1914, weighing 78 tons, foundered on 8th June 1942.
Dewey Eve	(ex Mary Swanston) 109 ton wooden drifter built by Herd & Mackenzie in Findochty (who also built the Rosevalley) in 1916, sunk in collision on 9th June 1940 and has just been located nearby the F2 & YC21.
Imbat	Drifter built in 1935, weighing 92 tons, sunk in collision on 4th December 1941.
Legend	Drifter lost in Scapa Flow on 28th December 1942 (cause unknown)
Ruby	Harbour support vessel built in 1902, weighing 46 tons, wrecked in gale in Scapa Bay on 9th October 1942.

The Drifter Lucy seen here depicted in a postcard produced in Germany was typical of the small fishing boats requisitioned by the Admiralty for tasks within Scapa Flow

AORANGI

The Aorangi sunk as a blockship near the Numidian

⊗ **Location:** Near the Holm church yard at Canniesile east of Kirk Sound.

😎 **Depth:** 12-14m (40-46ft)

🌀 **Conditions:** Clean sandy seabed, sheltered and non-tidal.

⊘ **Special Considerations:**
An awkward entry from the shore, better by dive boat.

➔ **Access:** From the shore or by boat.

🕐 **Diver experience:**
Suitable for all levels of diver.

The *Aorangi* was a former New Zealand Line passenger steamer weighing 4,268 ton, built in Glasgow in 1883, she was 118.5m (389ft) long and registered in Dunedin, New Zealand. Requisitioned by the admiralty, she was towed to Scapa Flow and sunk as a Blockship nearby the *Numidian* at Kirk Sound on 4th September 1915. She was subsequently raised in August 1920 in an exercise to clear the channel to allow for navigable shipping once more. However her term afloat was short lived as she broke her moorings and floated off out to sea where she lies today. Her boilers, bow section and part of her stern still remain, as does much of her hull, covered in seaweeds and surrounded by fish. There are some interesting swimthroughs under the hull and in all, it is quite a pleasant wreck dive with much to offer.

The Aorangi with her distinctive bows before she sank for a second time

COAL BARGE

(X) **Location:** Two-thirds of the way from the north of Rysa Little towards Lyrawa Bay on Hoy.

Depth: 8-10m (27-33ft)

Conditions: Muddy seabed.

(!) **Special Considerations:**
Very muddy bottom, great for scallops.

(→) **Access:** By boat only.

Diver experience:
Suitable for all levels of diver.

CONCRETE BARGE

(X) **Location:** Midway along the north shore of Flotta between the main jetty and Calf Sound.

Depth: 16m (54ft)

Conditions: Muddy seabed.

(!) **Special Considerations:**
Very little to be seen and not worth the effort due to the amount of silt in the water column.

(→) **Access:** By boat only.

Diver experience:
Suitable for Intermediate divers.

Lyrawa Bay and the north of Rysa Sound were used in WWI as the mooring location for the coal barges. These small and sturdy steel and wooden craft plied the waters daily, fuelling the Home Fleet. Nothing is known of the circumstances of her sinking, other than the fact that she is there. The barge was discovered by Kevin Heath whilst scallop diving and the position was reported to the Admiralty Hydrographic department at Taunton. The barge is of steel construction with two compartments, one fore, the other aft. Her hatch covers are open. She has quared off ends and rather rectangular in shape and is around 18m (60ft) long and sits 2 .5 m (8ft) off the seabed. There are plenty of plumose anemones on her as well as feather starfish; sea-squirts; swimming crabs and even scallops inside the open hold. There is surprisingly little algae growth on the ship, making her remarkably clean looking. There is usually a school of juvenile sprats swimming over the superstructure.

Gordon Ridley states in *Dive Scotland Volume III* that this barge was possibly French in origin, but that very little is known about her. Once thought to have been used by Metal Industries for salvaging the German Fleet, she was used as a British naval supply barge for a number of years and sunk at her moorings after being abandoned. Topped with kelp and with her sides covered on plumose anemones, she is a real little oasis of marine life in an other wise dull seabed area. Sadly no-one dives this lump anymore, particularly when there are such great dives nearby!

It should be noted that there are at least another eight similar barges dotted all over Scapa Flow, particularly in the Flotta, Rysa Little, Cava, Hoy arena where most of the British fleet would lay in anchor waiting for these sturdy little craft to supply them with coal and other provisions. Barges were also used by the salvors of the German fleet, for moving machinery as well as keeping position over the sites whilst lifting operations commenced.

HMS ROEDEAN

(X) **Location:**   In a sheltered area between the Point of Hackness at South walls and Crockness on Hoy.

(~) **Depth:**   15m (50ft)

(~) **Conditions:** No current but has a muddy seabed.

(!) **Special Considerations:**
There is some ferry traffic in the area, so care should be taken. The seabed and wreckage are covered in a layer of fine silt and visibility will inevitably be reduced with a number of divers exploring the site.

(→) **Access:**   By boat only.

(~) **Diver experience:**
Suitable for all levels of diver.

Launched as the TSS *Roebuck* in 1897, the *Roedean* weighed 1,200 tons and was built by the Naval Construction and Armament Company at Barrow and launched in 1897. She was 85m (280ft) long and operated as a ferry between Weymouth and the Channel Islands for many years. Her two coal-fired, three cylinder, triple-expansion engines pushed her along at a sprightly 19 knots. She was commandeered by the British Admiralty in 1914, converted into a minesweeper and fitted with two 12 pounder guns; it was then that she was renamed the *Roedean*. She was supposedly sunk by a German U-Boat in January 1915, but in actual fact she struck a mine (possibly an allied mine!).

Deemed a navigation hazard for many years, she was cleared in 1953 and 1956 and much of her superstructure is now gone. Obvious parts are the two massive boilers which lie amidships, large cable drums and mooring bollards near the stern. The visibility can be quite poor here and the muddy covering of the wreck soon gets stirred up by the divers' attention. Nevertheless, this is an interesting dive and if you have the chance and are in the area, why not try it!

Spools of cable encrusted in marine life lie on the seabed near the Roedean

MV JAMES BARRIE

⊗ **Location:** In Hoxa Sound midway between Flotta and Hoxa Head.

⊙ **Depth:** 35-42m (117-146ft)

◉ **Conditions:** Slight current over the clean gravel bottom.

① **Special Considerations:**

This dive can only be done at slack water as the currents here are fierce. The experienced dive boat captains time the dive religiously and will give you the maximum slack water possible, however current should be expected at all times! Sea angler fishing lines are also around the wreck, so watch out for hooks.

→ **Access:** By boat only.

◔ **Diver experience:**

Advanced recommended.

The *James Barrie* was a former Aberdeen built - Hull Fishing Vessel 40m (120ft) long, weighing 666 tons. She was on her way through the Pentland Firth when she struck Louther Rock on 27th March 1969. Taking on water, and thinking that the vessel was unable to be saved, the 21 crew abandoned ship on 29th March. However, in the early hours of the next morning, she floated off the rocks by herself and was adrift in the Pentland Firth. The Kirkwall Lifeboat *Grace Patterson Ritchie* was called to the scene accompanied by two Orkney fishing boats; the *Kildinguie*, skippered by John Dennison and the *Achilles*. The Lifeboat took her in tow by the stern, but could make little headway, so the *Kildinguie* attached ropes to the bow to keep her in place for the tow.

Magnus Dennison on board the fishing boat told me that the *James Barrie* had been holed in her net store but that the water leek had been held back by the ice which the *James Barrie* had in her forward hold. Gradually the packed ice melted and the sea water rushed through into the now empty hold. The crew quickly cut the lines, lest they be dragged under and only six hours after the *James Barrie* refloated herself, she sunk in under a minute.

COURTESY OF MAGNUS DENNISON

The final plunge of the MV James Barrie

Now lying on her port side in 42m (146ft) she is still intact. She has a large wheelhouse which supports the promenade deck and railings and behind that are all the fishing net winches. Forward are huge hatch covers now swung outwards; the hatch is navigable but at that depth time is limited to only a cursory examination. All of the metalwork is covered in algae and hydroids, as well as some dead men's fingers and plumose anemones. There are large schools of saithe and pollack on the wreck as well as the usual ballan wrasse.

MV MARA

⊗ **Location:** In Gutter Sound approximately 150m (500ft) from the F2 and YC21.

◉ **Depth:** 18m (94ft)

◉ **Conditions:** Slight current over the silty bottom.

⚠ **Special Considerations:**
Penetration of this wreck is not recommended as much of the wooden interior has collapsed.

➔ **Access:** By boat only.

◔ **Diver experience:**
Suitable for Intermediate divers.

COURTESY OF ANDY CUTHBERTSON

MV Mara in Stromness Harbour

The *M.V. Mara* was formerly a fishery research vessel which operated along the west coast of Scotland. Laterally, she became a live-aboard dive boat once owned by George Litts. She was sadly ignored due to lack of business and abandoned in Stromness harbour for a number of years and it was decided to tow her over to Lyness. Gradual deterioration over several winter storms occurred and she started to sink at her moorings. Deemed to be a navigation hazard, she was removed and pulled over to central Gutter Sound and sunk in 1995.

At only 22m (72ft) long, she is easily explored on a single dive. Relatively intact and covered

Part of the Mara's winch

in a fine patina of anemones and hydroids, she has a marked list of about 30 degrees to starboard. Her softer deck railing boards have rotted away, but her wheelhouse is still intact and her engine intake pipes still stand upright behind the wheelhouse. The interior of the wheelhouse is quite clean, but all of her portholes were removed whilst she lay at Lyness. She is absolutely surrounded by thousands of schooling juvenile fish as well as the usual wrasse species which accompany you on the dive.

PRUDENTIA

⊗ **Location:** West of Kirka Taing on Fara, midway towards Flotta.

◉ **Depth:** 22m (72ft)

◉ **Conditions:** No current, but has a silty seabed.

⚠ **Special Considerations:**
Although the wreck is not a war grave, the Orkney Islands Council Harbours Department state that she is off-limits to divers. The reason given is that she is too close to the Flotta Oil Terminal.

➔ **Access:** By boat only.

◔ **Diver experience:**
N/A.

The *Prudentia* was a fleet auxiliary tanker, chartered to supply the British Naval fleet during WWI. She was built in Middlesborough in 1889 by Palmers & Co. and was owned by the Leonards Carrying Company Ltd. She was 95m (320ft) long and weighed 2,731 tons.

There are two stories around her sinking. One is that she dragged her anchor and became fouled in the *Iron Duke's* mooring lines and buoy and then sank; the other story and in reality is that she struck the 5,200 ton *SS Hermioine* and quickly sank. A recent diving survey shows that she lies on her port side and is relatively intact with her main mast still attached amidships. She is able to be penetrated but leaks oil and her hull is smothered in sand and cement bags to stop the leaks. As the Prudentia is not a restricted vessel, it is hoped that diving will soon be able to be permitted on her, as she is at a perfect depth for a second dive and still relatively intact.

ROSEVALLEY (EX SILT)

⊗ **Location:** Opposite Rotten Gutter at the end of the airport runway at the bottom end of Weddel Sound.

◉ **Depth:** 12-16m (40-54ft)

◉ **Conditions:** Muddy seabed.

⚠ **Special Considerations:**
This is a lovely little dive, great for marine life and scallop hunting.

➔ **Access:** By boat only.

◔ **Diver experience:**
Suitable for all levels of diver.

(ex Silt) The *Rosevalley* was built for the Admiralty in Findochty in 1918. This small wooden vessel was 27m (87ft) long and weighed only 100 tons. She was then sold to Mr. A Jack, had a name change and used as a fishing boat, operating out of Aberdeen until she was requisitioned by the Admiralty for use transporting torpedoes during WWII. During very bad weather on 16th December 1943, she was involved in a collision and quickly sank; all of her deck cargo of torpedoes was recovered. She is still upright, but only the wooden stern, steel wheelhouse and large boiler are evident, all the rest is well broken up.

The Rosevalley

STRATHGARRY

⊗ Location: Midway between Quoy Ness on Flotta to Hoxa Heade on South Ronaldsay.

Depth: 57m (194ft)

Conditions: Strong current over the gravel bottom. Slack water here is one hour after slack water on the James Barrie.

⚠ Special Considerations:
This wreck is in the main oil tanker movement area and permission must be obtained from the Orkney Islands Council Harbours Department on the day of diving.

➔ Access: By boat only.

Diver experience:
Suitable qualified advanced divers only.

The *Strathgarry* was built in Aberdeen in 1906 by Hay, Russel & Co. Ltd. and weighed 202 tons. She was originally owned by the Aberdeen Trawling and Fishing Company and skippered by Captain I McFarlane. She was 34m (113ft) long and 6.7m (21.9ft) wide and her 67h.p. three cylinder, triple expansion engine pushed her along at a mighty 11 knots. The *Strathgarry* was requisitioned by the British Admiralty during WWI. There is some controversy over the sinking of this single deck steam trawler as she was possibly struck by *HMS Herald* and lives were lost on the *Strathgarry* when she sank. Whatever the case, this is a deep dive and should not be considered lightly. In fact, with the wreck remaining relatively intact and upright, listing slightly to port, she is often used as a training dive for trimix divers. The hull is complete and the wheelhouse

structure is still fairly intact and you can see the steering helm quite clearly. Much of the wooden decking has all fallen in and you can see into the depths of the ship. The marine life is pretty much the same as that found on the *James Barrie* with hydroids; dead men's fingers; plumose anemones; brittle starfish and lots of small fish darting around.

The metal parts of the superstructure are now a mass of plumose anemoses due to the almost constant tidal stream through this passage.

UB116

⊗ **Location:**   Northwest of Quoy Ness on Flotta

⊚ **Depth:**   28m (94ft)

⊚ **Conditions:** Slight current over the silty bottom.

① **Special Considerations:**

> There is some boat traffic in the area, so care should be taken. The seabed and wreckage are covered in a layer of fine silt and visibility will inevitably be reduced with a number of divers exploring the site.

➔ **Access:**   By boat only.

🕑 **Diver experience:**

> Intermediate to advanced recommended.

On 28th October 1918 the *UB116* approached Scapa Flow through Hoxa Sound under the command of Kapitänleuntant Hans-Joachim Emsmann. At 181ft long, the submarine was a type UB111 class, carrying 10 torpedoes, one deck gun and thirty-four crew. It is curious that Emsmann made his early approaches on the surface and then submerged; it was as if he wanted to be seen. However, the only way to make entry into Scapa Flow was to submerge to negotiate the mines and nets. Sadly he had not counted on the hydrophones which were also placed in Hoxa Sound and they were quickly detected; the mines were detonated electronically from the shore and the *UB116* was destroyed. The location of the submarine was found the next morning by two trawlers using the new echo-sounding equipment known as ASDIC. A local tale told that tapping could be heard coming from the inside of the submarine, but regardless of this, the destroyer on duty bombed her again with depth charges.

Royal Navy salvage divers (known as Tin Openers) led by the indefatigable 'Dusty' Miller investigated the wreck the next day and found three bodies in the conning tower, then gained access into the boat through the fore hatch and cleared the way through to the control room, hampered by two torpedoes in their racks and the bodies of sailors jammed in the buckled bulkhead door. Curiously, Miller reported that they could only find crew in officers' uniforms and that there were suitcases full of civilian clothes leading to speculation that the crew may have been bringing in the submarine to surrender almost at the end of the war.

The *UB116* lay unnoticed for many years until construction began on the crude oil and gas pipeline to service the new oil terminal on Flotta. The submarine must have made for an early interesting dive but the *UB116* was sold for scrap in 1969. The Navy removed the remains of the bodies and attached charges to her torpedoes and she was blown up in 1975, the blast was so great that it shattered windows in homes on Flotta.

Now located at the entrance to Pan Hope Bay off Flotta in a depth of 28m (94ft), on a fine silty seabed, the wreckage is pretty well flattened and much of it now sunk beneath the seabed. Her partly hidden conning tower is about the only recognizable feature, the rest is just junk, covered in fine marine growth, brittle starfish, sea urchins and plenty of small fish.

Right: The UB116 is now almost flattened but is in a very contained area and easy to explore on one dive

The F2 at sea

World War II Wrecks

Much of the emphasis on the wreck diving of Scapa Flow has been placed squarely on the shoulders of the German Fleet scuttled back in 1919, however there is a German ship from WWII sunk near the Lyness Visitor centre on the Island of Hoy. A salvage company tried unsuccessfully to remove her guns. (Sorry, they were successful in removing her guns, they placed them into the hold of their salvage barge, but the barge sunk due to a combination of bad weather and incompetence) So now there is an additional shipwreck lying alongside the *F2*. All of the Orkney Dive Boat Operators will visit the site as it is usually done in conjunction with a lunchtime stopover at the Museum. The *F2* was an experimental ship captured early on in the war and was taken to Scapa Flow to decide what to do with her next. One local story tells of a group of erstwhile salvors removing some interesting bits of brass from her engine room. Apparently one piece of brass was a particularly important part and the ship subsequently sunk at her moorings!

A surprising number of small craft were also lost during the WWII years and these were primarily harbour support vessels, small fishing boats, coal barges and boom defence craft. These sinkings were usually the result of collision with other (larger) admiralty vessels. A few of these are dived regularly and information on one such as the Rose Valley can be found on page 80

It is fair to mention here that other famous sinking in Scapa Flow in WWII, and that is the loss of *HMS Royal Oak*. Left to defend the Orkneys, Kirkwall and the remaining British Fleet, the *Royal Oak* was attacked mercilessly and sunk on October 13th 1939, just six weeks into the war, by the German submarine *U-47*. *HMS Royal Oak* is a designated War Grave and no diving is allowed on her or in the vicinity.

Left, The bows of the F2 are covered in marine life

F2 + YC21

(X) **Location:**

Northeast of Lyness Pier on Hoy, midway in the channel.

(≈) **Depth:** 16m (54ft)

(●) **Conditions:** Slight current over the silty bottom.

(!) **Special Considerations:**

There is some boat traffic in the area, so care should be taken if you stray from the site. Most divers also visit the salvage barge YC21 as they are so close together and are achievable as a single dive. The silt is a major factor in the hold of the YC21, so stay well clear.

(→) **Access:** By boat only.

(⊜) **Diver experience:**

Beginner to Intermediate recommended, no wreck diving skills are necessary.

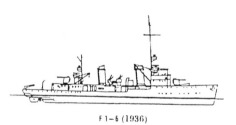

F 1−6 (1936)

Line drawing of the 'F' series escort boats

The *F2*, although a German escort boat, similar to a Light Cruiser is actually a casualty of WWII. Built at the Germaniawerft Shipyard in Kiel, she was 79m (263ft) long and displaced 756 tons and completed in 1936. At the start of the war, she was converted into a Torpedo Recovery Boat but was captured during an early skirmish at the start of the war and taken to Scapa Flow where she was moored in Gutter Sound. She sank at her moorings in 1946.

The *F2* is now a very popular dive, lying on her port side, the shallowest part to her hull is only 8m (27ft) near where her anchor chain comes out of the hawse. The front end of the ship is fairly intact all the way back to just aft of the bridge. One of her forward guns is still in position. The seabed is littered with debris and there are lots of cuckoo wrasse to follow you around. A large roll of steel cable lies next to the hull and her deck bollards, cleets and capstan are clearly visible. She was purchased by Metrec Engineering in 1967 to be salvaged. The mid to aft sections of this ship are now utterly destroyed in the search for the non-ferrous metal from her. Her stern post is still intact, but that is the only point of interest and is not worth the swim to investigate.

Connected by a 30m (100ft) line is the salvage barge *YC21*. This wooden barge weighed 550 tons and was used specifically in the salvage of the *F2*. In November 1968, shortly after the twin 20mm anti-aircraft guns had been removed from the *F2* and placed in the barge's hold a storm blew up. The crew lashed the barge to the *F2*, but had not accounted for the rising tide or the height of the waves. The barge sunk at her moorings and is now a welcome addition to a rather ordinary wreck site. Relatively intact, the barge sits upright and her wooden hull is deteriorating. Now eaten by shipworm and other marine organisms, she is well covered in marine life. In her hold can be found the 20mm gun from the *F2* and on each side of the hold can be found the electric generator and workshops used in the salvaging of the *F2*. Both wrecks together are worthy of one dive and should really only be classed as such.

Right: The 20mm gun from the F2 inside the hold of the YC21

HMS Royal Oak photographed shortly after her anti-submarine attack 'blisters' were fitted.

Breaking the Flow Defences

HMS ROYAL OAK

The green channel buoy warns divers of unauthorized diving in HMS Royal Oak's vicinity

HMS Royal Oak is perhaps the most documented of the war graves and indeed the author has been honoured to attend several *Royal Oak* Survivor's Association meetings and has been very privileged to be allowed special permission on several occasions from HM Admiralty to accompany members of the Royal Navy Clearance Diving Unit to dive on *HMS Royal Oak* on the anniversary of her sinking.

The author's photographs of the oil leaking from the hull were instrumental in the decision to try and drain the ship of oil, oil which has been seen on the surface of Scapa Flow since that fateful incident in 1939.

Left, HMS Royal Oak during manoeuvres in Scapa Flow.

This leaking oil, visible on the surface is a permanent reminder of the loss of HMS Royal Oak

One of five Revenge class of battleships, *HMS Royal Oak* was built in the Naval dockyards at Devonport in Plymouth and was commissioned in May 1916. At over 188m (660ft) long, 28m (94ft) wide and a hull of 8.5m (28.5ft) depth. She displaced 29,150 tons and was capable of speeds in excess of 20 knots driven by 40,000 horsepower oil-fuelled marine turbines. *HMS Royal Oak* was also equipped with the largest array of guns ever fitted to a British battleship having eight 15-inch (384mm) guns set in four pairs, which were capable of firing one ton (1000kg) shells over 13miles (21km). With a compliment of over 1250 men to keep her at battlestations, the *Royal Oak* first saw action at the Battle of Jutland and was credited with two hits.

Stationed for the most part in Scapa Flow, the *Royal Oak* was also involved in the Mediterranean patrol and was berthed at Grand Harbour, Valletta in Malta. As the increase of the arms race was to develop, and the recognised vulnerability due to submarine attack, it was decided that anti-submarine attack 'blisters'

would be fitted to the sides of the *Royal Oak*. Sadly these not only reduced the battleship's cruising speed down to 14knots, they were to prove entirely inadequate in the early morning of October 14th 1939.

Suffering from engine troubles and combined with her low speed, it was decided that *HMS Royal Oak's* new duties would be to protect Kirkwall and the main bases around Scapa Flow in case of aerial bombardment. The Fleet's flagship *HMS Iron Duke* was stationed near Lyness and *HMS Pegasus* was also moored close by. The day before, virtually the entire fleet had been ordered out of Scapa Flow by Admiral Forbes due to the increasing danger from aerial attacks as Luftwaffe reconnaissance flights had been detected several days before. It was feared that Scapa Flow could be a 'bottle-neck' should there be a major aerial attack. The latest German aerial photographs indicated that the bulk of the British North Atlantic fleet was still anchored in Scapa Flow and an immediate assault was brought forward.

The reconnaissance photographs also indicated that the Blockships to the east of Scapa Flow had largely deteriorated, particularly in Kirk Sound (also known as Holm Sound). Other ships had started to be sunk with the *Soriano* in March of 1939; the *Cape Ortegal* at Skerry Sound in September and the *Madja* at Water Sound earlier that year in February. More ships had been ordered but they were either not ready to be placed, or had not been prepared by Metal Industries for sinking.

Commodore Döenitz decided to give one of the younger and more daring submarine captains, Günther Prien, the opportunity to try and penetrate the base once more. His submarine, the *U47* had already seen action and was responsible for the sinking of the *Bosnia*, the *Claro* and the *Gartavon* on the 5th, 6th and 7th of September, that year. On receipt of the survey to find Scapa Flow's weakness, Commodore Döentiz said *"I hold that a penetration at this point (Holm or Kirk Sound) on the surface at the turn of the tide would be possible without further ceremony"*. Little hope of success was thought of, but Günther Prien was to prove how inadequate the British defences were and make one of the most controversial attacks ever recorded in the annals of naval history.

Gunther Prien The German submarine commander responsible for sinking HMS Royal Oak is seen here on the conning tower of his submarine, the U47

The artist Rico's superb impression of HMS Royal Oak as she is today

Prien approached Scapa Flow through the narrow approaches at Kirk Sound and although the way was hampered by the Blockships, the tide was high and the entrance had still not been completely blocked and entered Scapa Flow with surprisingly little difficulty a little after midnight. His route shows that he first sailed towards Lyness where the bulk of the fleet would have lain at anchor, along with the flagship *HMS Iron Duke*. Finding no ships in the area, but also encountering no resistance, he turned to the north and spotted three ships at anchor. These were *HMS Royal Oak*, *HMS Pegasus* and possibly *HMS Iron Duke*.

When the first two torpedoes struck the *Royal Oak* at one 0'clock in the morning, the dull thud confused the crew of the *Royal Oak* into thinking the muffled explosions were an on-board problem and certainly not a U-Boat attack. This gave Commander Prien an additional 20 minutes in which to return to his firing position, reload and fire a second salvo which gave three direct hits amidships. Such was the ferocity of the explosions that the ship healed over alarmingly and all of the lights went out. That night, it had been fine weather and all of her hatches were open, her guns were unlocked and when the ship rolled over, her gun barrels rolled round and further pulled the ship beneath the surface. Water crashed through the open hatches and the men asleep in their bunks were unable to get out in time. Fire ripped through the ship igniting the cordite and all inflammable products and munitions it could find. Thankfully many men managed to scramble out onto the ship, covered in oil, burned, bleeding and distraught. It took only

ten minutes to send the *Royal Oak* to the seabed taking with her the lives of 833 officers and men. Many of the men are buried in the Royal Naval Cemetery at Lyness on the Island of Hoy.

The mighty guns of HMS Royal Oak sadly aided her sinking

The *U-47* quickly made her escape from Scapa Flow and managed to avoid detection. On returning to her home base at Wilhelmshaven on the 17th of October, they were given a hero's welcome and Lieutenant Prien was awarded the Knights Cross of the Iron Cross First Class by Adolf Hitler. When the *U-47* left Germany, she used to have a drawing of a skull and crossbones wearing a top hat on the conning tower (which was thought to represent the

The U47's victorious return to Germany

attack to the death by the *U-47's* crew to the might of Neville Chamberlain), when she returned to Wilhelmshaven the *U-47* now depicted a 'snorting' bull and henceforth was known as "The Bull Of Scapa Flow".

[There is some confusion over the *U47's* report as they said that they thought possibly the *Iron Duke* was *HMS Repulse*. We also understand that much of their 'official' report was doctored by German Intelligence Services to create a new German Hero in Günther Prien. We know that the *Repulse* left that day with the rest of the fleet, we also know that Prien insists that he hit another ship that same night. The British Admiralty never confirmed that the *Iron Duke* had been hit when the *Royal Oak* sunk, however we do know that the *Iron Duke* was heavily listing to port and beached at Lyness

with a twenty foot hole in her bows when a Luftwaffe squadron of four Junkers-88 of the 1/K.G.30 group attacked three days later on the 17th of October. We also know that their bombs missed. So, where and when did the Iron Duke get hit? A report by Metal Industries however tells a different story, the report clearly indicates that Metal Industries were engaged in pumping out the *Iron Duke* and patching the hull when they were attacked the day after the sinking. One can only surmise that it was deemed too sensitive an issue to report that the British Atlantic Fleet's Flagship had also been possibly torpedoed the same night that the *Royal Oak* was lost.

Just one week after the sinking of the *Royal Oak*, the *Lake Neuchatel* was sunk in Kirk Sound on 21st October. Following this, the *Gambhria* was sunk in December, thus effectively closing off all other passage through the Sound. As a direct result of the loss of the *Royal Oak*, Winston Churchill visited the scene and immediately ordered the complete blockage of all the sounds to the east of Scapa Flow. Four barriers were to be built in all, with the 'help' of Italian Prisoners of War. These are still known to this day as the Churchill Barriers.

A series of anti aircraft guns from HMS Royal Oak

The gun barrels of HMS Royal Oak are covered in plumose anemones

HMS Royal Oak now rests on her starboard side, but almost upside down in 32m (107ft) of water. Her keel comes to within 5m (17ft) of the surface and is camouflaged by a thick layer of marine growth including kelp; feather starfish; plumose anemones; swimming crabs and soft corals (known locally as 'dead men's fingers'). Unlike the great German Fleet Battleships hulls, which are in a ruinous state, the *Royal Oak's* upturned hull is intact and has the appearance of an underwater cliff.

When you reach the port railings at 16m (54ft) you must swim out and away from the hull, to avoid descending into the labyrinth of twisted metal. The seabed is at 32m (107ft) and the Admiral's Steam Pinnace lies intact alongside the great ship, pulled under when she sank. The visibility deteriorates rapidly as you approach the ship as the rust particles and other debris now hang like a permanent shroud around the ship. Further out onto the seabed can be found those sections of the hull, mastheads, spotting top and conning tower which were ripped off when this massive ship hit the bottom.

The copper Carley Life Rafts were pulled under when the Royal Oak sank and unable to help in the sailors' escape

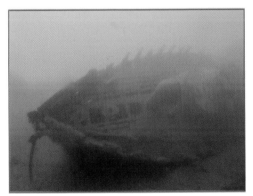

The Admiral's steam pinnace lies intact and alongside HMS Royal Oak

Each year, on the anniversary of the sinking of the ship, members of the Royal Navy Northern Diving Unit make their annual pilgrimage to ceremoniously unfold the battle ensign and once more fly this flag from the stern of the *Royal Oak* to the memory of those 833 men who lost their lives. The battle ensign is

attached to the port propeller shaft which is now located in a depth of 15m (50ft). The year old ensign is removed and cleaned. This is then presented to the Royal Oak Survivors Association and then passed on to various groups of servicemen and organisations who were represented on the *Royal Oak*. The *Royal Oak* is one of the most intact sunken battleship in the world and ranks as the top shipwreck in European waters and one of the top six in the world. *HMS Royal Oak* is a designated war grave and is protected by Navy Law. Diving on her or in her vicinity is strictly forbidden.

The location of the wreck is nearby the Scapa Bay green channel buoy. On the buoy is a plaque which reads THIS MARKS THE WRECK OF HMS ROYAL OAK AND THE GRAVE OF HER CREW. RESPECT THEIR RESTING PLACE. UNAUTHORISED DIVING PROHIBITED."

The Italian Chapel on Lamb Holm

Orkney Italian Chapel

As a direct result of the sinking of *HMS Royal Oak* by Gunther Prien and the *U-47*, First Lord of the Admiralty, Winston Churchill visited Orkney and reviewed the existing blockship barriers at each of the sounds to the east of Scapa Flow, Particularly where the *U-47* had managed to pass in and out of Scapa Flow through Kirk Sound. He decreed that permanent barriers were to be contructed to totally block the eastern approaches and to render Scapa Flow a much safer anchorage for the Home Fleet.

The contract for the work was awarded to Balfour Beatty, but due to conscription, there were not as many workers to find for the task. Italian Prisoners of War, captured during the North African campaign were enlisted for the task and over 1350 Italians were transported to Orkney and billeted in 'nissan huts' on the Island of Lamb Holm.

Rather cheerless and lacking in home comforts, the Italians, whilst working alongside civilians on the construction of the barriers, set about improving their huts by laying concrete paths, planting flowers and of course redecorating. Italian artist Domenico Chiocchetti created a sculpture of St.George slaying the Dragon, built on a framework of barbed wire covered in cement. However the lack of a proper chapel was deeply felt. Chiocchetti, along with a small band of helpers set about creating a sanctuary in one of the huts and totally transformed the interior and built a new façade to hide the original outline of the hut. A blacksmith named Polumbi created a rood screen and gate and others constructed the concrete altar, replaced all the electrics and plastered the interior. The glass windows were painted to represent St. Francis of Assisi and St. Catherine of Sienna and inspired by a picture of the Madonna & Child, Chiocchetti set about painting the interior and transforming it into a Chapel.

Left: The Italian Chapel was fully restored by her original artist Domenica Chiocchetti

The Italian prisoners were repatriated in 1945, after the war, but Domenica Chiocchetti stayed on to complete his labour of love. Sadly it was eventually neglected, but was regarded as a national treasure. A Preservation Committee was formed in 1960 and Chiocchetti was tracked down to Moena, a small village in the Dolomites and invited back to Orkney as a guest of the Preservation Committee and spent three weeks lovingly restoring the chapel to its former glory.

Before he left Orkney, he wrote this letter to the People of Orkney:

> Dear Orcadians –
>
> My work at the chapel is finished. In these three weeks I have done my best to give to the little church that freshness which it had sixteen years ago. The chapel is yours – for you to love and preserve. I take with me to Italy the remembrance of your kindness and wonderful hospitality. I shall remember always, and my children shall learn from me to love you. I thank the authorities of Kirkwall, the courteous Preservation Committee, and all those who directly or indirectly have collaborated for the success of this work and for giving me the joy of seeing again the little chapel of Lamb Holm where I, in leaving, leave a part of my heart. Thanks also in the name of all my companions of camp 60 who worked with me.
>
> Goodbye dear friend of Orkney – or perhaps I should say just "au-revoir".

COURTESY OF ORKNEY MUSEUM & ARCHIVES

Domenica Chiocchetti died at his home in Moena on 7th May 1999, aged 89. The Italian Chapel is open to everyone.

(Courtesy of Orkney Museum Archives)

The Italian POW Camp Band

This painting by Domenica Chiocchetti shows the POW's at work on the Churchill Barriers

Each year the Ensign flies from the stern of HMS Royal Oak as a mark of respect to the lost.

War Graves

HMS Royal Oak is undoubtedly the most talked about and indeed the most revered of the British naval war graves, but there are another two naval war graves in Orkney, one outside Scapa Flow off western mainland and the other just north of the oil terminal on the island of Flotta.   These ships, the *Hampshire* and the *Vanguard* both had catastrophic loss of life almost within one year of each other during World War I

Part of the assembled crew of HMS Royal Oak, many of these men would perish that fateful night.

HMS Hampshire on maneuvers in Scapa Flow

HMS HAMPSHIRE

Whilst *HMS Hampshire* is not located in Scapa Flow, but rather off Marwick Head along mainland's rugged west coast, the *Hampshire* certainly deserves a mention in this publication.

After the successful outcome over the Battle of Jutland, the British Admiralty returned to their main base at Scapa Flow. It was agreed that although Germany's naval fleet had taken a resounding blow, there was little to stop their expansion into Russia. If Germany could seize the northern ports, they would be able to slip by the British blockade. Britain's Minister of War, Field Marshall Lord Kitchener and his staff were dispatched to Archangel in Russia to help shore up Russia's defences. Despite advice not to take the westerly route out of Scapa Flow and around northern Orkney due to the known threat that the German submarine, *U-75* had been seen in the vicinity and had placed 34 mines in the main sea lanes. Despite this and coupled with worsening weather conditions, the 10,850 ton *Hampshire* left Scapa Flow on 5th June 1916, just one week after the Battle of Jutland. Sadly, after only a short time at sea, it is presumed that the *Hampshire* struck a mine and blew up west of Marwick Point. Only 12 seamen were to make it to the shore out of 655 officers and men.

Great controversy ensued over the loss of the *Hampshire* and many conspiracy theorists blamed the loss as an assassination of Lord Kitchener, as he had been openly criticised for his war tactics. The theory proliferated when the Stromness lifeboat was not allowed to attend the scene to aid in the search for survivors and locals were turned back at bayonet point when they tried to help the survivors on the shore. It has been said that German, Irish or even British secret agents had sabotaged the *Hampshire*. Lord Kitchener was a dramatic and heroic figure and there was not one person in the British Isles who did not recognise his photograph, as it had been used in the conscription posters.

HMS Hampshire was lost with 643 men including Lord Kitchener. Lord Kitchener was a popular, if not controversial figure during WWI

The Kitchener Memorial now stands in a superb RSPB Reserve

Whatever the reasons for the tragic loss of this fine ship and all those men, the *Hampshire* now lies in 60m (200ft) of water off Marwick Head. Several teams of divers have visited the site over the years and one survey group stated that they had found evidence that the Hampshire had indeed struck a mine. However the scale of the destruction to the ship, now scattered on the seabed may dictate otherwise. No-one will know for sure and *HMS Hampshire* is now declared as a war grave and no unauthorised diving is permitted on her. One of her propellers is now on display at the Lyness Visitor Centre. A Memorial Tower to Lord Kitchener sits atop the cliffs at Marwick Head, near the scene of the loss.

HMS VANGUARD

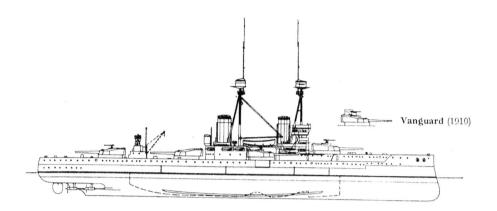

Vanguard (1910)

HMS Vanguard

HMS Vanguard was one of the first of the new style of Dreadnought Battleships known as the St. Vincent class to be built in the Vickers shipyards at Barrow-in-Furness. She carried ten 12-inch / 50 calibre guns mounted in twin gun turrets, three of which were arranged amidships. Powered by two sets of Parsons marine engines which drove four propellers, she could reach speeds in excess of twenty knots. During the Battle of Jutland, the *Vanguard* used her guns for the first time in active combat and was 16th in line of Jellico's assigned 24 Dreadnoughts. After this action, the *Vanguard* spent almost all of her time in Scapa Flow, apart from a few skirmishes and exercises.

On 9th July 1917, she had been out on exercise during the day and returned to her usual moorings off the northern shores of Flotta. A number of her officers left the ship to attend a concert on board *HMS Royal Oak* which was moored up in Scapa Bay. Suddenly, just before midnight, the sky was lit up by a simply earthshaking explosion which ripped through the *Vanguard's* ammunition magazine. Fuelled by cordite a pall of black smoke shot through with bright orange flames illuminated the Scapa Flow skyline. One of her 400 ton gun turrets actually landed in a farmer's field on Flotta over a mile distant and nearby ships had to quickly clear off the *Vanguard's* burning debris, lest their own ships caught fire.

Apart from the ninety-five officers and men who had been off the ship, only three survivors were found out of 804 men who perished. Not surprisingly, further rumours of sabotage proliferated when letters written in German, a German Bible and even a photograph of a German lady were discovered amidst the wreckage. It was also discovered that the civilian ordnance fitter (who had just left the ship) was the same fitter who had been on *HMS Natal* when she blew up under almost identical circumstances in the Cromarty Firth in 1915. The *Vanguard* was extensively salvaged by

Nundy Marine Metals and her remains now well broken up in 34m (114ft) of water, recognisable sections are still apparent, particularly the stern whish also has a three-pounder gun on her. *HMS Vanguard* is officially designated as a War Grave and no unauthorised diving in allowed on her, or in the general vicinity.

HMS Vanguard was lost mysteriously with 804 lives

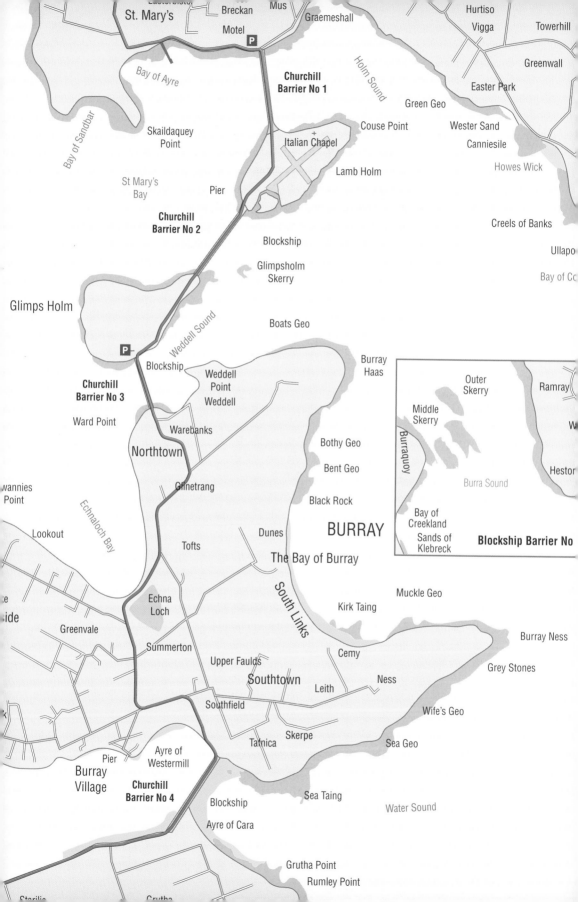

Churchill Barriers

When war broke out on 4th August 1914, Admiral Sir John Jellico quickly recognized the vulnerability of this great harbour. Jellico, whose official title was Admiral Viscount Jellico of Scapa, authored several books, including *The Grand Fleet, The Crisis of the Naval War* and *The Battle of Jutland Bank*. He was now in command of over 100 naval ships, and whilst Scapa Flow was the best naval base available, there were problems with the overall security. These were exacerbated when the German submarine *U-18* entered Scapa Flow on 3rd November 1914. Unsuccessful in her raid, the U-Boat was later rammed by the trawler *Dorothy Grey* and she later beached on the Pentland Skerries. This direct action prompted Jellico to move the fleet headquarters to Longhope. They later moved to Lyness on Hoy.

Jellico increased the coastal defences to cover Hoxa, Switha and Hoy Sounds to the south with anti-submarine netting and indicator loops (a type of early hydrophone) to listen for enemy craft underwater. He also implemented the plans for sinking derelict shipping to block the entrances to the five vulnerable sounds to the eastern and western approaches. Over a two year period at the start of WWI, twenty-three ships were sunk in five different locations: Kirk Sound (also known as Holm Sound); Skerry Sound; East Weddel Sound; Water Sound and Burra Sound.

As early as March 1915 Admiral Colville remarked that the present system of Blocking Ships combined with boom defences and attendant trawlers was particularly costly and that "they could not be considered very satisfactory or be compared with the safety afforded if the channels leading into Scapa Flow could be blocked by concrete blocks or by some sort of dam." This early report to the admiralty also addressed the situation and probable effect of the tidal flow through Hoxa Sound from a navigational point of view, should the east and west channels be blocked. He further suggested that "some big contractor" be sent to Scapa to recommend how the sounds could be permanently blocked as he thought that the long term cost of such a project would be more than compensated by the current cost of guard destroyers; armed trawlers; boom defences and personnel and obviate the necessity of Hoy and Holm batteries; personnel and accommodation.

This type of Blocking Ship or Blockship protection proved extremely successful in the short term, but the inevitable deterioration of the Blockships led to an Admiralty inspection in June, November and December 1915 and September 1916, where the remains of the Blockships were sketched by Captain B.M. Chambers R.N. and an analysis made on each ship sunk.

After the war, a number of these ships were salvaged and when three local fishermen lost their lives when their small fishing boat struck one of the submerged ships, urgent measures were called for the removal or dispersion of the existing Blockships. The entrance at Kirk Sound was cleared sufficiently by refloating the *Aorangi* and pulling the *Numidian* parallel to the shore, to clear the channel for local fishing boats to pass through. All other ships were left in place and thought that they would provide sufficient protection to Scapa Flow and deter any submarine access into the base of the Home Fleet.

Leading up to the outbreak of World War II, the British Admiralty decided to reinstate the Blockships and ordered the sinking of a further 24 ships although they only sunk 22. However the Treasury placed a spend limit of only £10,000 per ship and actually refused one suitable ship because it was over priced at

£12,000. A report was submitted in May 1939 that "not another penny" was to be spent on the Blockships for Scapa Flow. Now that this plan was in place, the Admiralty was again rather complacent, thinking that no hostile boat would dare to try and attack Scapa Flow, rather that any attack would be by air. However, the inspection report sent in by the survey vessel *H.M.S. Scott* in May 1939 clearly stated Kirk Sound perfectly navigable with a channel over 400 ft wide and a depth of over two fathoms at low tide, 4m (13ft). The Admiralty chose to ignore this report, or certainly did not act on it immediately, as Blockships had been ordered for placement. The Controlled Mining Base Ships *Manchester City* and *Ringdove* had been ordered for deployment and would carry out the sinking of the first Blockships.

This almost arrogant assumption that Scapa Flow would not be attacked by another enemy submarine was proven entirely inadequate a second time when the German U-Boat, the *U-47,* commanded by Günther Prien stole into Scapa Flow just six weeks after the start of WWII in 1939. He negotiated the 'zig-zag' channel through Kirk Sound, scraping between the *Thames* and the *Minieh* and struck two British naval ships including *HMS Royal Oak*, which quickly rolled over and sank, taking with her 833 officers and men. As a direct result of this attack, Winston Churchill visited Orkney and ordered the construction of permanent barriers across the entrances to the four eastern passageways into Scapa Flow.

Sir Arthur Whitaker, Civil Engineer-in-Chief to the Admiralty surveyed the sites aboard his survey vessel *HMS Franklin*. From there, a scale model was quickly built at Manchester University to check the water and tidal flow variations and garner an approximation of what would be required for 'fillin in the sea'. Not only were the tidal races to be stemmed, a road was also to be built on the barriers to link Mainland with Lamb Holm, Glimps Holm, Burray and South Ronaldsay.

The contract for the work was awarded to Balfour Beatty, and various sub contracts were awarded to local companies. The southern section of Barrier IV was subcontracted to William Tawse & Co. of Perth. The barriers were designed and supervised by Sir Arthur Whitaker and his directions were carried out by H.B. Hurst who was then succeeded by C.K. Johnstone-Burt, Herbert Chatley and J.A. Seath. Until 1942, the resident civil engineer was E.K. Adamson. From 1942 to the barrier completion the resident superintending civil engineer was G. Gordon Nicol whose notes and photographs survive today through Orkney Archives in Kirkwall.

Balfour Beatty worked very closely with the British Admiralty as well as the salvage company Metal Industries and on May 10th 1940, the 15,551 ton liner *SS Almanzora* arrived off Holm Sound carrying all the necessary equipment to start the construction site, including a couple of Thames barges, the *Roman* and the *Gatville*. Work was long, hard and difficult in those northern latitudes.

There was a distinct lack of manual labourers for this rather daunting task, as many able-bodied men had been conscripted into the armed forces. It was decided that Italian Prisoners of War, captured during the North African campaign could possibly be used to help in accomplishing this task. Over 1350 Italians were eventually transported to Orkney with the first 600 prisoners of war marshalled at Edinburgh's Waverley Station under the command of Major J.C.Yates, from there they transferred to Aberdeen docks where they boarded a boat for Orkney in January 1942. In total, 800 Italians were stationed on the Island of Burray and a further 550 on Lamb Holm.

Blockships lying alongside newly a newly completed Churchill Barrier

The prisoners of war outnumbered the local work gangs two to one and very quickly gained the respect and admiration of their captors.

New piers were constructed at each end of the barrier positions to help in the movement of massive blocks of stone and tons of gravel from Moss Quarry. Massive gantry cables were strung across the treacherous rapids and sunken Blockships and gradually the barriers were extended across between the islands creating dramatic waterfalls and rapids as the rising and falling tide continued to beat against these new defences.

These cables were 2 inches in diameter and were controlled by winchmen who handled the 'travellers' or carts that dumped rock spill from above, at the same time a small railway was extended out onto the advancing barrier. This had side tipping carts, that way, there were two

A number of the old bolsters, or concrete moulds are still to be seen at the edge of causeway, these actually formed over 51,000 blocks and spanned four stretches of water, to a depth of over 18m (60ft) in some places

differing methods for the construction to advance. Once sufficient infill was in position and the sea was being held back, the cables or 'blondins' shifted and dropped 4.8 ton blocks. Heavier 10 ton blocks were moved by railway cart.

Barrier I across Kirk Sound was completed by August 1943 and Barrier III was completed by September. It would be another year before all of the barriers would be in place and they were officially opened on 12th May 1945 by the First lord of the Admiralty. (Ironically just in time for the end of the war!) The project cost more than the Two Million Pounds Sterling awarded for the contract, it also cost the lives of ten men, seven by drowning. The Materials used included the following: 522,330 cubic yards of rock; 117,724 steel bolster nets; 34,384 5ton concrete blocks; 15,036 10ton concrete blocks; 2,206 4.8 ton concrete blocks; 6 acres of tarmac were used to surface 2.5km (1 mile) of causeway road and 3.2km (2 miles) of connecting road.

The bulk of the Italians had already left Orkney the previous September as all of the heavy work had been completed, however a few stayed behind to assist Domenico Chiocchetti to complete the work on the chapel in the converted Nissan Hut on Lamb Holm. The Italians had not only proved themselves able workers, many were now great friends of the islanders. It was with some sadness when the bulk of the workforce eventually left and returned to their homelands. Not only had they built great barriers to prevent enemy shipping from ever again entering Scapa Flow from the eastern approaches, they changed the lives of the residents on the southern islands forever, by providing the means of a safe road link to the Orkney mainland and forego the necessity for travelling by boat.

THE BARRIER BLOCKSHIPS

This section has been perhaps the most difficult to unravel, as there is so much information and misinformation out there. However I am indebted to the massive amount of work and research done by the many different authors who have published their accounts in previous publications. To get the correct positions of the Blockships, archival photographs were examined in detail through Orkney Library Archives; aerial photographs taken by the Admiralty and Ordnance Survey; artist's drawings and site plans of the sinking of the first barrier Blockships in 1914/1915 and Admiralty Hydrographic maps, plans and photographs from both World Wars. These details were perhaps the most telling as they quickly put the sites into a correct perspective. Kevin Heath also helped immensely; his knowledge of the Blockships is astonishing to say the least. Ben and Sarah Wade of Scapa Scuba were also instrumental in garnering rough drawings of the underwater positions of the wrecks at Barriers II and III. Naval records as well as the actual inventory of the Blockship preparation work carried out by Metal Industries, prior to their sinking, proved to be a godsend. Soon, differing information quickly emerged particularly the spelling of many of the ships' names. Anomalies soon arose, such as the size of the *Ilsenstein,* British Naval records show her as weighing 8,216 tons, almost 7,000 tons more than her previous estimates (hardly surprising so much of her still remains!). Other records had the *Doyle* (read *Moyle* in several transcripts) sunk in Burra Sound in 1940 during WWII, however she was actually sunk on 7th October 1914. These and many more points have come to light, hopefully the following list will help readers gain a better view and understanding of these remarkable shipwrecks.

The eastern approaches have been irreversibly transformed by the construction of the Churchill Barriers.

THE BLOCKING SHIPS OF WORLD WAR I AND WORLD WAR II

(Please note that in the following descriptions, only those that are still worth visiting have specific dive information included, all others have only a brief history)

Name	Location	Date Sunk	Notes
AC6 Barge	Skerry Sound	1941	Raised then later scrapped
Almeria	Skerry Sound	1915	Scrapped and lost under sand
Aorangi	Outside Scapa Flow	1915	Still diveable
Argyll	Skerry Sound	1914	Scrapped, but her boiler can still be seen
Budrie	Burra Sound	1915	Blown apart, not dived
Busk	Kirk Sound	1940	Scrapped and raised
Cape Ortegal	Skerry Sound	1939	Still diveable
Carolina Thorndén	Water Sound	1942	Raised and sold
Carron	Water Sound	1940	Lost under sand, part of mast still visible
Clio I	Water Sound	1914	Scrapped and raised
Clio II	East Weddel Sound	1915	Swept out to sea, east of Barrier III
Collingdoc	Water Sound	1942	Partly scrapped, lost under sand, part of bridge still visible
Doyle	Burra Sound	1914	Still diveable
Elton	Skerry Sound	1914	Scrapped in place and now under other blockships
Emerald Wings	Skerry Sound	1940	Still diveable
Empire Seamen	East Weddel Sound	1940	Still diveable
F/C Pontoon	Skerry Sound	1941	Still diveable
Gambhira	Kirk Sound	1939	Raised and eventually sunk off Llandudno
Gartmore	East Weddel Sound	1915	Still diveable
Gobernador Boreis	Burra Sound	1914	Still diveable

Gondolier	Water Sound	1940	Lost in gale, buried under sand east of Barrier IV
Ilsenstein	Skerry Sound	1940	Still diveable
Inverlane	Burra Sound	1944	Finally collapsed, still diveable
Juniata	Inganess Bay	1940	Raised and was lost a second time, snorkeling recommended
Lake Neuchatel	Kirk Sound	1939	Scrapped and raised
Lapland	East Weddel Sound	1915	Scrapped and covered by Barrier III
Lorne	Water Sound	1915	Scrapped, blown apart and lost under Barrier IV
Lycia	Skerry Sound	1941	Scrapped in place, only engine block remains
Madja	Water Sound	1939	Scrapped and lost under sand
Martis	East Weddel Sound	1940	Still diveable
Minieh	Kirk Sound	1915	Still diveable
Numidian	Kirk Sound	1914	Still diveable
Pontos	Water Sound	1914	Lost under sand
Redstone	Kirk Sound	1940	Scrapped and raised
Reginald	East Weddel Sound	1915	Snorkeling recommended
Reinfeld	Skerry Sound	1914	Scrapped in place and remains are lost under sand
Ronda	Burra Sound	1915	Blown apart, not dived
Rosewood	West of Barrier II inside Scapa Flow	1914	Still diveable
Rotherfield	Burra Sound	1914	Blown apart, not dived
Soriano	Kirk Sound	1939	Scrapped and raised
Tabarka	Kirk Sound Burra Sound	1941 1944	Originally sunk in Kirk Sound, she was raised and sunk again, still diveable
Teeswood	Skerry Sound	1914	Scrapped, but some parts remain
Urmstone Grange	Burra Sound	1914	Blown apart, not dived

DIVING THE BLOCKSHIPS

The average depth along the Churchill Barriers is around 8m (27ft) on the seaward side and 12-21m (40-70ft) on the Scapa Flow side. The prevailing weather conditions will determine which side of the barriers to dive, but in actual fact, there is little choice on where you will dive. All of the wrecks are now well broken up, some through natural causes, others by salvage. Many are hardly worth the effort and others are now completely hidden underneath that old cliché 'the sands of time'.

Much of the wreckage now lying alongside the Churchill Barriers is scattered over a wide area and for the most part either covered in silt or kelp. The average depth of the sounds on the eastern side are around 8m (27ft) deep, but does reach as deep as 21m (70ft) in the former deep tidal channel at Kirk Sound. The larger wrecks are still evident on the eastern side of the Barriers, particularly Barrier II where the *Lycia's* engine block, *Emerald Wings'* mast and the top of the *FC Pontoon* are visible at all states of tide. The *Reginald* is the most obvious at eastern Barrier III and whilst she is not described here as a dive, I know of several people who have enjoyed snorkelling around her open interior. The biggest changes have taken place at Barrier IV across Water Sound, where virtually nothing remains of the Blockships there: part of the *Carron's* mast sticks up through the sand, a small piece of the *Pontos* can be seen near the top of the *Collingdoc's* concrete bridge, sadly this is all that can be seen of that once fine ship, now surrounded by a sea of grass. The water's edge is almost 90m (100yds) from the roadway and by all accounts, the entire eastern bay of Water Sound will eventually fill with sand. Churchill Barrier No.4 has irrevocably altered the marine ecosystem in this area of Orkney, subsequently no diving takes place here.

Many divers tend to dive on the more sheltered western side of the barriers and visit ships such as the *Numidian; Thames* and the *Minieh* off Barrier I and the *Empire Seamen* and *Martis* off Barrier III. However, the best diving by far is on the eastern side of Barrier II, where the *Lycia; Ilsenstein; Emerald wings; FC Pontoon; Cape Ortegal; Argyll* and the *Reinfeld* are located in only 8m (27ft) of water.

Sadly there are no visible Blockships at Burra Sound to the west of Scapa Flow now, as the once superb remains of the *Inverlane* have disappeared below the onslaught of that punishing tidal race. However the three remaining Blockships underwater, the *Doyle; Gobernador Boreis* and the *Tabarka* are widely regarded as three of the top dives in Scapa Flow.

CHURCHILL BARRIER 1 – KIRK SOUND (HOLM SOUND)
WORLD WAR I BLOCKSHIPS

As already mentioned, the diving on Barrier I is concentrated on the western side of the barrier and whilst the three Blockships still in evidence are manageable from the shore, most divers do these wrecks by charter boat. The *Aorangi* is still diveable to the east of the barrier, but very few boats ever go there due to its location, however it can be done as a shore dive, should you really wish to visit this old hulk. The dive is described in the "Other Wrecks" section.

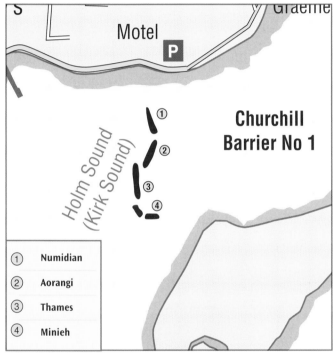

Blockships sunk during World War I

AORANGI ②

The 4,268 ton former Union Steamship Company vessel was 118.5m (389ft) long and built in Glasgow in 1883. Registered in Dunedin, New Zealand, she was chartered by the RAN in August 1914 to act as a supply ship for the fleet and was fitted with a 12-pounder gun. She was not commissioned into the Navy but continued to be manned by her civilian crew. The *S.S. Aorangi* took part in operations against the German colonies in the Pacific until she was returned to her owners in May 1915, after which she was passed to the British Admiralty. She was sunk as a Blockship at Scapa Flow naval base on 4th September 1915. She was raised in August 1920, broke her moorings and floated off out to sea where her remains now rest near the Holm church yard at Canniesile, however, all archives state that the *Aorangi* remained in merchant service until scrapped in 1925!

The Aorangi sunk in position at Barrier 1

MINIEH (EX ALSATIA) ④

(X) Location: Lying in a southeasterly direction on the western side of Barrier I, south of the Thames.

Depth: 7-18m (23-60ft).

Conditions: No current to speak of; but can be quite dark on the morning dives.

(!) Special Considerations:
There is a heavy covering of silt everywhere and the deeper sections are now completely covered, it is recommended to keep your distance from this area when examining it.

(→) Access: Can be done from the shore, but it is more comfortable by boat.

Skill Level: Beginner to Intermediate, but some wreck diving experience is preferable, as this dive is the most complicated of all the Barrier Wrecks.

108.8m (357ft) long; 2,890 ton steamer built in Glasgow in 1876, sunk on 27th February 1915. She quickly broke her back in the deep channel and stayed in place, located to the south of the *Thames,* Günther Prien actually mentioned this Blockship and the *Thames* during his incredible raid on the *Royal Oak* in October 1939, The *Minieh* only had minimal superstructure salvage undertaken.

The *Minieh* is the deepest of all the Blockships in the eastern barriers as it was sunk over the deep scour trench of the tidal flow. The ship quickly broke her back, with the ship virtually folding in half and her midships stuck in the channel. When the Admiralty inspection was carried out in 1915, the artist clearly depicted her fore and aft masts leaning in towards each other. The ship is well broken up now and

much of her lower sections are covered in fine sand and silt as the tidal race was stemmed with the construction of the first barrier. There is quite a large jumble of wreckage in the trench, but recognizable sections of her boilers, masts, bollards, anchor winch etc are plainly visible. Generally made as a boat dive at the same time as the *Thames*, the top superstructure is covered in seaweeds and kelp.

Approaching the Minieh

NUMIDIAN ①

⊗ **Location:** Lying in a northwesterly direction almost adjacent to shore and is the most northerly of all the Blockships.

🌀 **Depth:** 7-12m (23-40ft).

🌀 **Conditions:** No current, wreck is well broken up and covered in silt and kelp.

! **Special Considerations:**
There is heavy deterioration and much of the superstructure is quite jagged, it is recommended to keep your distance from this area when examining it.

→ **Access:** Can be dived from the shore, but it is more often accessed by boat.

🌀 **Skill Level:** Beginner to Intermediate.

4,836 ton former Alland Line Trans Atlantic passenger ship, 121.9m (400ft) long and built in Glasgow in 1891, sunk on 30th December 1914. The most northerly of the Blockships, she was pulled parallel to the shore in 1919 to allow boat traffic to reuse this entryway after three local men were drowned when their small fishing boat struck an underwater obstruction. The *Numidian* was one of the first Blockships to be sunk in Kirk Sound, and also one of the first ships to be scrapped after the First World War. Salvaged to her keel by East Coast Salvage Company in 1924. When Balfour Beatty started construction on the barrier, they employed Metal Industries to remove much of her metal plate to use in repairs etc. The remains of the ship have settled into the fine sand and shell debris and all of her metal parts are now covered in seaweeds. There are very few recognizable parts left now, but the ship is usually teaming with fish including schools of juvenile pollack and saithe. The usual species of wrasse are always present and the hulk is home to several large lobsters and crabs. This dive is usually done as a shore dive as it is so close to the edge of the barrier.

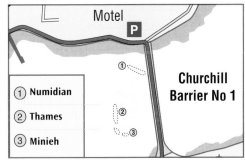

① Numidian
② Thames
③ Minieh

Motel

Churchill Barrier No 1

Parts of wrecks visible in 2005

Numidian being scrapped

THAMES ③

(X) **Location:** Lying in a southerly direction between the Numidian and the Minieh and lies parallel to Barrier One.

(☺) **Depth:** 7-12m (23-40ft).

(☺) **Conditions:** Can be choppy in a westerly wind and lower sections are covered in silt and mollusk shell debris.

(!) **Special Considerations:**
There is heavy deterioration of the ship after it was salvaged and the time factor has taken its toll on this once proud ship, so care must be taken with regards snagging expensive equipment and dive suits.

(→) **Access:** Can be done as a shore dive, but more commonly by boat.

(☺) **Skill Level:** Beginner to Intermediate, but some wreck diving experience is preferable.

Aerial view showing Numidian, Thames and Busk

1,327 ton former Royal Mail Steam Packet Company steamer, 132.9m (436ft) long and built in Glasgow in 1887 and registered in Grangemouth, sunk on 7th January 1915. Extensively salvaged with her stern and all top superstructure removed, but she is still in place and lying parallel to the Barrier, to the north of the *Minieh*, on the Scapa side of the barrier.

The former Royal Mail Steam Packet Company steamer *Thames* had once been commanded by Admiral Jellicoe's father, but she would end her days in Scapa Flow. She was a graceful three masted, steamer with two funnels and a clipper bowsprit. She was sunk, by blowing her bottom out, subsequently she settled upright, mid channel and looked like she was still sailing. Largely scrapped, she now has the appearance of lying on her side, as the metal plates are all twisted and bent over. A number of portholes are still obvious, but all of the lower sections are covered in a thick layer of silt and an adverse kick of the fins quickly reduces the visibility. The uppermost metal parts are covered in various seaweeds, sadly there are few recognisable parts anymore and you tend to use the wreck only as a marker to dive on the more interesting *Minieh* to the south.

by Captain B.H. Chambers R.N Dec. 8 1915.
NUMIDIAN   AORANGI   THAMES   MINIEH

WORLD WAR II BLOCKSHIPS

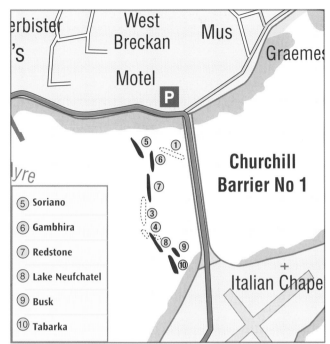

5 Soriano

6 Gambhira

7 Redstone

8 Lake Neufchatel

9 Busk

10 Tabarka

Blockships sunk during World War II

BUSK **9**

367 ton single screw steamer built in North Shields in 1906 and registered at Whitehaven in Cumbria, sunk on 17th February 1940. Broke up during a gale that first winter and her hull was removed, very little remains now.

GAMBHIRA **6**

(ex War *Merlin*) 5,257 ton steamer built in Sunderland in 1910, sunk on 8th December 1939. Salvaged and refloated in 1943 and used as an ASDIC target ship in Liverpool Bay and eventually sunk off Llandudno.

LAKE NEUCHATEL **8**

(ex *Renfrew*; ex *Claveresk*; ex *Houstone*; ex *Mari*; ex *Ulversmead*) 3859 ton Royal Navy Special Service Vessel built in Sunderland in 1907, sunk on 21st October 1939. Largely salvaged by Metal Industries in 1948, very little can be found of her.

REDSTONE **7**

(ex *Margari*; ex *Orbe*; ex *Wye Crag*) 3,110 ton single screw steamer built in West Hartlepool in 1918 and registered in London, sunk on 2nd May 1940. Removed and scrapped by Metal Industries.

SORIANO **5**

(ex *Evansville*; ex *Lake Tahoe*; ex *SNA 4*) 3,543 ton steamer built in Michigan and registered in Montevideo, Uruguay and sunk on 15th March 1939. Acquired by the British Admiralty at the same time as that other Great Lakes ship, the *Collingdoc*. She was salvaged and removed by Metal Industries.

TABARKA **10**

(ex *Pollux*) 2,642 ton steel, single screw steamer built in Rotterdam in 1909 and registered in Rouen, seized by the British Admiralty off Falmouth in 1940 and sunk on 23rd March 1941. Refloated in 1944, moved and sunk in Burra Sound.

CHURCHILL BARRIER 2: SKERRY SOUND

Barrier II is by far the most popular of all the barrier diving locations and is suitable for beginner divers with easy shore access direct onto the Blockships.   It is hardly worth mentioning the *Lycia* as a specific dive, as only her engine block remains.

However, a line stretches from her to the *Ilsenstein* and from there you can access the *Cape Ortegal* and the *Emerald Wings*.   It is debatable whether you can tell where one ends and another begins, but there are distinctive bows and propellers in various locations.   The *FC Pontoon* sits alone and can be visited on the same dive, or as part of a wider exploration dive.   The boiler of the *Argyll* to the south is also interesting, but hardly worth the effort of a specific dive; therefore it too is not described as a dive site in this section.   Many visiting divers and diving students have their first dives on the shipwrecks at Barrier II.

WORLD WAR I BLOCKSHIPS

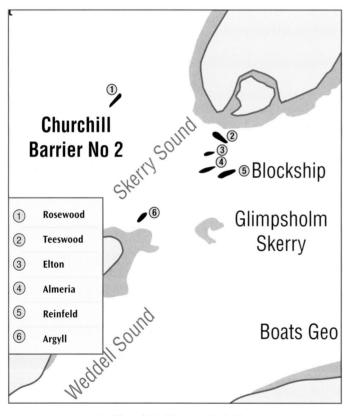

Position of World War I Blockships

ALMERIA ④

(ex *Wakefield*) 2,418 ton steamer, 89.3m (293ft) long built in Sunderland, sunk on 20th February 1915. Scrapped by Metal Industries, what used to be left of her is now below the sand between the Ilsenstein and the Emerald Wings.

ARGYLL ⑥

1,185 ton steamer, 73.8m (242ft) long built and registered in Hull, sunk on 17th September 1914. She quickly broke in two, forwards; her large boiler can be seen at the southern edge on the seaward side of the barrier, the rest of her was salvaged and her lower hull parts are now beneath the sand.

ELTON ③

2,461 ton steamer, 91.4m (300ft) long, built and registered in West Hartlepool in 1880 and sunk on 3rd October 1914. By 1915, her back was broken and she was upside down, scrapped extensively, only her engines and some hull plates remain; the *Ilsenstein* and *Emerald Wings* were placed on top of her.

REINFELD ⑤

(ex *Ramses*) 3,634 ton steamer, 103.6m (240ft) long, built in Newcastle in 1893 and registered in Hamburg and sunk on 2nd October 1914. Furthest east of all the Blockships, she was scrapped by Metal Industries, what was left of her is now below the sand northeast of the *Emerald Wings*.

Divers prepare to dive the Blockships at Churchill Barrier 2

TEESWOOD ②

(ex *Westwood*) 1,589ton steamer 85m (279ft) long built in 1882 and sunk on 19th September 1914. She drifted off position whilst being sunk and ended up adjacent to the northern shore and hence no use as a Blockship. Her stern is very close to the northern corner on Barrier II, adjacent to the engine block of the *Lycia*. She was scrapped by East Coast Salvage Company in 1924.

ROSEWOOD (EX BLAKEMORE) ①

(X) **Location:** About 300m (1000ft) southwest of the pier at Kirk Point, well out into the Scapa Bay area.

(👃) **Depth:** 6-8m (20-27ft).

(🌊) **Conditions:** Little to no tidal action, but the site is quite exposed to northerly and westerly gales.

(!) **Special Considerations:**
Quite silty, so care should be taken when swimming around the remains of the hull.

(→) **Access:** By boat only.

(🤿) **Skill Level:** Beginner to Intermediate, but some wreck diving experience is recommended.

Often overlooked by the lure of the Blockships closer to the barriers, the *Rosewood* was built in South Shields in 1889 and sunk on 18th September 1914. Although the single screw steamer weighed 1,757 ton and was 79.2m (260ft) long, the Navy tried to blow her bottom out unsuccessfully and she drifted into the sound on an incoming tide before she sank. Largely scrapped on site by various companies and locals, she now rests on a silty seabed in 8m (27ft). Her boilers and much of her stern section are intact and the sides of her hull still stand quite proud. The area is known for having plenty of fish, so take care of discarded fishing lines around the hull.

WORLD WAR II BLOCKSHIPS

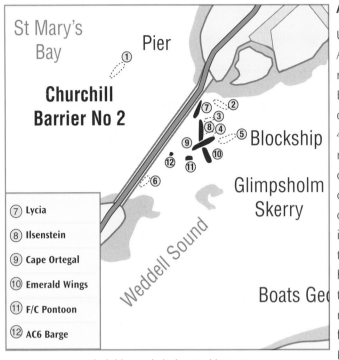

Blockships sunk during World War II

St Mary's Bay
Pier
①
Churchill Barrier No 2
⑦ ②
③
⑧ ④
⑨ ⑤ Blockship
⑫ ⑩
⑪
⑥
Glimpsholm Skerry
Weddell Sound
Boats Ge

⑦ **Lycia**
⑧ **Ilsenstein**
⑨ **Cape Ortegal**
⑩ **Emerald Wings**
⑪ **F/C Pontoon**
⑫ **AC6 Barge**

AC6 BARGE ⑫

Used by Metal Industries for Admiralty Fleet work and repairs, due to the lack of Blockships ready for deployment, she was sunk on 4th August 1941. Some reports have her as completely broken up and confused with some of the other wreckage in the immediate area, however there is some indication that her sinking was only temporary and that she was refloated later and used for a few more years by Metal Industries before being scrapped, certainly there is little evidence of her now.

LYCIA ⑦

2,338 ton motorship built in Port Glasgow in 1924, sunk on 19th February 1941. The most distinctive of all the Blockships high and dry at the northeastern end of Barrier I, she was scrapped on site by Metal Industries and now only her massive engine block stands above the surface at the shore entry point for diving the wrecks.

Engine block of the Lycia

CAPE ORTEGAL ⑨

⊗ Location: Lying in a northeasterly direction between the Ilsenstein and the Emerald Wings.

👁 Depth: 7-12m (23-40ft).

🌀 Conditions: Wreckage is topped by various seaweeds and is a bit confusing with the proximity of the other wrecks in the vicinity.

⚠ Special Considerations: There are several large sections of wreckage where you can swim under but always check that your exit is clear before entering.

➔ Access: Done as a shore dive combined with the other wrecks in the same location.

🐟 Skill Level: Beginner.

Cape Ortegal Propeller

of the winter gales. Although much of her more interesting parts are now buried under the sand, her stern section and upturned propeller are quite interesting and have created a swimthrough where these parts can be accessed. Following on from the stern, the direction takes you southwest towards the *FC Pontoon*.

This former 4,896 ton steamer built in Glasgow in 1911, was sunk just five days after the start of the war, however she did not last long as a Blockship because she was unballasted and quickly rolled over and broke up during the first

Lamb Holm, photographed from Glimps Holm, showing the blockships in position and the steel cables used in dropping the concrete blocks

EMERALD WINGS ⑩

Location: Directly out and continuing on from the *Ilsenstein*.

Depth: 0-12m (0-40ft).

Conditions: Usually calm, but can be a little surge in an easterly gale around the top of the superstructure.

Special Considerations: Penetration is not recommended in the forward section near the standing mast.

Access: Done as a shore dive, often as part of a wider exploration of the wrecks.

Skill Level: Beginner.

(ex *Nicolaos Baikos*; ex *Deputé Pierre Goujon*) The mast standing at an oblique angle above the waters at Skerry Sound is from the *Emerald Wings*. Built in Cherbourg in 1920, this 2139 ton steamer was sunk on 13th July 1940

extending the line of Blockships from the shore southeast towards the rocky reef known as Glimpsholm Skerry where they were connected by cables to the old beacon.

Although much of her stern section is confused with the Cape Ortegal, her midships and forward section are very interesting. Her boilers and other recognizable parts are covered in a light growth of kelp and other seaweeds.

Views of the Emerald Wings both above and below

124

F/C PONTOON ⑪

(X) **Location:** Lying in a southwesterly direction between the Emerald Wings and Barrier II.

(👁) **Depth:** 0-7m (0-23ft).

(👁) **Conditions:** Easy access through several sections of the pontoon's girders.

(!) **Special Considerations:**

There can be a little surge amidst the pontoon legs, but it is quite safe and is usually calm in the interior above the boiler.

(➔) **Access:** Usually as a shore dive at the same time as visiting the other wrecks.

(🐢) **Skill Level:** Beginner.

This Floating Crane Pontoon was used by Metal Industries for salvaging the shallower wrecks. Due to a lack of readily available Blockships, it was sunk on 22nd May 1941. Now without her crane, the distinctive rectangular structure with her open sides and huge internal boiler is still intact and sits partly out of the water to the south of the *Ilsenstein*.

For me, this former floating crane barge is the best of the Blockships found on this barrier.

Easily accessible from the shore, its distinctive rectangular box shape rises above Skerry Sound at any state of tide. Although the crane was removed, the barge's lattice-work support legs are open in several places allowing easy access for the diver into the interior. Here you can surface on top of the massive old boiler with its brass valves still intact and now covered in a patina of seaweeds and barnacles. The legs make for a great photographic backdrop.

The legs of the pontoon are covered in marine life

The remains of the FC Pontoon are still visible at any state of tide

The valves on top of the old boiler tank

ILSENSTEIN ⑧

(X) **Location:** Lying in southeasterly direction connected to the *Lycia* by a guideline.

(⊙) **Depth:** 5-11m (17-37ft).

(⊙) **Conditions:** Fine sand and little silt, but visibility is usually reduced.

(!) **Special Considerations:**
This is a pretty easy dive following the lines of the salvaged ship.

(→) **Access:** Directly from the shore next to the *Lycia* engine block.

(⊙) **Skill Level:** Beginner.

8,216 ton coastal freighter built in Kiel in 1889 and registered in Bremen. Acquired by the Admiralty, she was sunk to replace the then useless *Cape Ortegal* on 18th February 1940. Largely scrapped on site by Metal Industries as Barrier II neared completion, these are still the largest remains of any of the Blockships in the vicinity, her bows and railings are quite distinctive.

Connected by a line from the *Lycia* engine block, the aft section of the remains of this coastal freighter slowly rises out of the sandy seabed. Following salvage (read scrapped) there is little of any recognizable parts at first, just big flat plates and deck, however in the summer months these metal parts are covered in sea lettuce algae which is browsed upon by sea hares. As you travel down the edge of the

Sea Hare

hull, gradually more parts take shape until you reach the very distinctive bows with their metal railings. From here on in, it becomes a bit of a jumble as the sterns from the *Emerald Wings* and the upside down *Cape Ortegal* are all in this one location.

Above left and above: views of the Ilsenstein bows

The Ilsenstein shortly after she was sunk as a Blockship in 1940

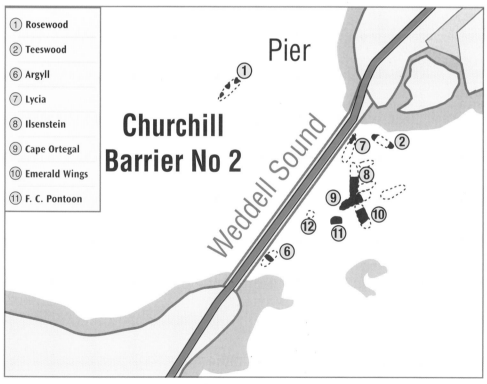

①	Rosewood
②	Teeswood
⑥	Argyll
⑦	Lycia
⑧	Ilsenstein
⑨	Cape Ortegal
⑩	Emerald Wings
⑪	F. C. Pontoon

Pier

Churchill
Barrier No 2

Weddell Sound

Parts of wrecks visible in 2005

CHURCHILL BARRIER 3: EAST WEDDEL SOUND

The Barrier across East Weddel Sound is located on quite a steep bend as it sweeps southwest along the south coast of Glimps Holm before turning 90 degrees southeast towards Burray. Your first view of the Barrier includes the former schooner *Reginald* which has basically stayed in the same position since the time she was sunk and rolled over. This barrier has the least number of Blockships, being the smallest and shallowest of all the former entrances into Scapa Flow. The *Lapland* was lost under the construction of the barrier and only part of the *Gartmore* remains. Both the *Empire Seamen* and the *Martis* sit proud of the water on the Scapa side of the barrier. The *Reginald* is located on the seaward side and is used by a local fish farm for anchoring their platforms. Former concrete box moulds are found at the southern section of the seaward side of the barrier.

WORLD WAR I BLOCKSHIPS

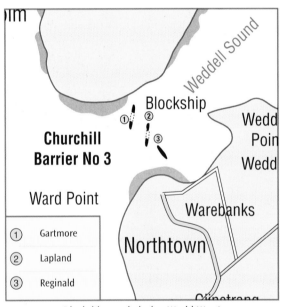

Blockships sunk during World War I

CLIO II

2,733 ton steamer, 70.1m (230ft) long, built in Hartlepool in 1889 and sunk on 27th February 1915. Well ballasted, the firing circuit failed and *Clio II* swept the channel and sunk well out to the eastwards and was deemed as no use as a Blockship. Often confused with the identical *Clio I* that was sunk ten months earlier at Barrier IV on 29th April, 1914.

REGINALD ③

930 ton schooner, 73.2m (240ft) long, built in Glasgow in 1878 and sunk on 15th September 1915. The only Blockship at this barrier located in the eastern approaches, the stern section of the ship, lying on its port side is one of the most distinctive of all the views of the exposed Blockships.

The exposed midships of the Reginald

GARTMORE ①

(X) **Location:** Lying in westerly direction between the northwestern shore access of Barrier III and the *Martis*.

(⊙) **Depth:** 5-7m (17-23ft).

(●) **Conditions:** Remarkably clean with very obvious ship parts to examine, visibility is usually reduced due to tidal action.

(!) **Special Considerations:**
There is very little of the wreck to be seen and most divers just use the wreckage as a marker for the *Martis*.

(→) **Access:** Can be made as a shore dive, but more commonly by boat.

(🐟) **Skill Level:** Beginner to Intermediate, but some wreck diving experience is recommended.

The single screw steamer Gartmore was built in South Shields in 1880 and weighed 1,564 ton. Requisitioned by the Admiralty, she was 82.3m (270ft) long, and sunk on 14th September 1915. As she was unballasted, she quickly broke in two with her stern at the shore and the remains of her bows pointing in a southwesterly direction and was little use as a Blockship. Accessible from the shore at the northwestern side of the barrier, the remains of her stern are quite close to the corner. Her propeller, propshaft and crankshaft are still visible in only 3m (10ft) of water and are remarkably clear of marine life. Divers tend to swim over this section to gain access to the much larger *Martis*.

LAPLAND ②

(ex *Dauntless*; ex *Ptarmigan*) 1,234 ton steamer 78m (256ft) long, built in Dundee in 1890, registered in Liverpool and sunk on 16th September 1915. Also unballasted when she sank, she quickly broke her back in the deeper part of the channel, but stayed in place. The construction of Barrier III virtually covered the ship and what could once be seen is rarely exposed due to sand build up.

An ordnance survey photograph of Barrier 3

COURTESY OF ORKNEY ARCHIVES

An oblique Admiralty view of Barrier 3 and her visible blockships

COURTESY OF ORKNEY ARCHIVES

BLOCKSHIPS SUNK DURING WORLD WAR II

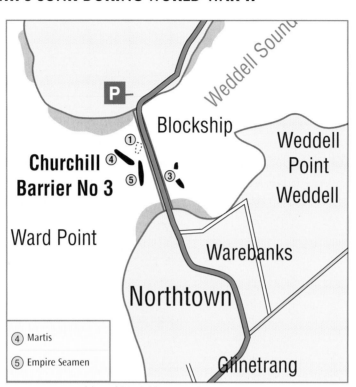

Position of blockships sunk during World War II

The Martis and Empire Seamen to the west of Barrier 3, the Reginald is to the east

EMPIRE SEAMEN ⑤

⊗ Location: Lying south of the *Martis* on the Scapa side and lies almost parallel to Barrier III.

⊙ Depth: 0-8m (0-27ft).

⊙ Conditions: Can be choppy in a westerly wind and lower sections are covered in silt and mollusk shell debris.

⊙ Special Considerations:
There is heavy deterioration of the ship, however it is quite open in aspect and quite easily negotiated.

➔ Access: Can be made as a shore dive, but more commonly by boat.

⊙ Skill Level: Beginner to Intermediate, but some wreck diving experience is preferable.

(ex *Morea*) 1,921 ton steamer built in Lubek; became part of a fleet of twelve vessels all with Empire as a prefix to their name, she was seized by the British Navy in the Bay of Biscay as she tried to run the British Naval Blockade of the German Ports and sunk as a Blockship on 30th June 1940. The *Empire Seamen* and the *Martis* are visible at all states of tide on the Scapa side of the barrier, with the *Empire Seamen* to the south of the *Martis*. The bows, stern and superstructure were removed by Metal Industries.

Her top superstructure was removed by Metal Industries as the barrier was gradually formed. As she was a relatively modern ship, much of her spare parts were used for repairs of naval and merchant marine shipping which were stationed in Scapa Flow. *The Empire Seamen* is possibly the most enjoyable of the Blockships at Barrier III as her hull and lower sections are all relatively intact allowing for fairly easy access through several large and cavernous swimthroughs. There is surprisingly little kelp growth in this area, but the holds and outside the hull are always full of pollack and the usual species of wrasse.

Wreck parts visible of the Empire Seamen in 2005

MARTIS ④

⊗ Location: Lying between the *Gartmore* to the north and the *Empire Seamen* to the south on the Scapa side of Barrier III.

⊙ Depth: 0-7m (0-23ft).

⊙ Conditions: Can be choppy in a westerly wind and lower sections are covered in silt and mollusk shell debris.

⊘ Special Considerations:
Quite open in aspect the ship has several swimthroughs, but care as always, should be taken in penetration.

➔ Access: Can be done as a shore dive, but more commonly by boat.

⊜ Skill Level: Beginner to Intermediate, but some wreck diving experience is preferable.

(ex *William Bell*) The *Martis* is the largest of the Blockships sunk at East Weddel Sound and was built in South Shields in 1894. Weighing 2,483 tons, this single screw steamer was sunk on 14th June 1940. Being much more visible that the *Empire Seamen*; she tends to be visited more by divers as she is closest to the northern entry point into the Scapa side of the barrier. Her bows, stern and superstructure were removed by Metal Industries as the barrier was constructed and it is the rectangular box-like section that divers like to explore due to the large open spaces and overhanging swimthroughs. There are always schools of fish in and around the wreck and the dive is usually well lit as the water here tends to be relatively clear. The bottoms of the holds are covered in silt however, so divers should practice an easy side kick to avoid stirring up the sediment.

The Martis

Wreck parts visible of the Martis in 2005

CHURCHILL BARRIER 4: WATER SOUND

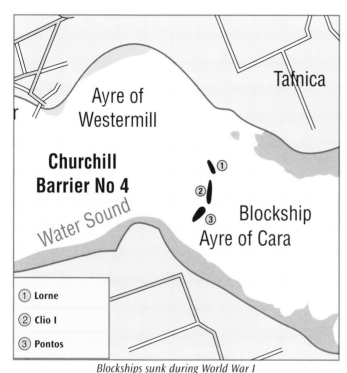

Ayre of Westermill

Tafnica

Churchill Barrier No 4

Water Sound

① Lorne

② Clio I

③ Pontos

Blockship
Ayre of Cara

Blockships sunk during World War I

WORLD WAR I BLOCKSHIPS

Sadly there is no diving to have at Water Sound, as the construction of the barrier has changed the ecosystem irrevocably. All of the Blockships are now under the sand and only a few straggly remains can still be recognized. It is only through the Admiralty plans and archive photographs that we can even identify these parts and the ships that they are still attached to.

CLIO I ②

2,733 ton steamer, 70m (230ft) long, built in Hartlepool in 1889 and sunk on 29th April 1914. Well ballasted, she stood upright and served her purpose well as a Blockship for many years until she was scrapped by Metal Industries prior to the construction of Barrier IV. She was located between the *Lorne* to the north and *Pontos* to the south and faced in a SSE direction. Often confused with the identical *Clio II* that was sunk ten months later at Barrier III on 27th February 1915.

LORNE ①

A 73.5m (241ft) 1,186 ton single screw steamer built in Hull in 1873 and registered in Southampton, sunk on 17th September 1915. Pointing in a northwesterly direction, she was sunk mid-channel and concrete ballasted to keep her in position. The northern section of the channel was closed off with boom netting attached to a buoy. She was partly scrapped, as well as being blown apart by explosives and what was left was partly hidden under the barrier as construction commenced, some parts may have been confused with the *Clio I*.

PONTOS ③

(ex *St. John City*; ex *Clan Macnab*) This 93m (305ft) long, 2,265 ton steel, single screw steamer was built in Glasgow in 1891 and registered in Andros, Greece, sunk on 30th November 1914. Positioned at the southern approaches to the channel and pointing in a southwesterly direction, she quickly broke her back and was largely scrapped over the intervening years. For a long time, her remains could be viewed leading off from the stern of the *Collingdoc*. Sadly whatever remains of her now has been lost beneath the rising sand dunes along the eastern side of the barrier.

Aerial views of Barrier IV, Water Sound

WORLD WAR II BLOCKSHIPS

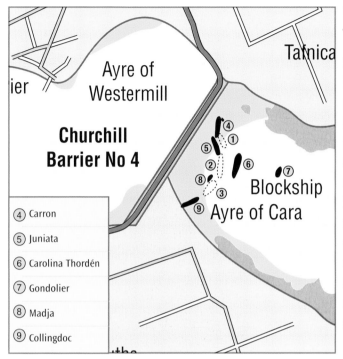

Blockships sunk during World War II

CAROLINA ⑥ THORDÉN

3,645 ton motor tanker, built in Sweden, registered in Helsinki and bombed off the Faroes. She was taken in tow by the Admiralty and sunk on 8th April 1942 to replace the *Gondolier*. All accounts indicate that she was salvaged, raised and sold off, as there is no long term evidence of her at the Water Sound Causeway, indeed all of the aerial photographs examined exclude her.

The only recognizable part left of the Carron is part of her lower steel mast.

CARRON ④

(ex *Glasgow*) 1,017 ton steamer, built in Dundee in 1894 and registered in Grangemouth, sunk on 3rd March 1940. The most northerly of the Blockships sunk at Barrier IV, she was salvaged by Metal Industries as work commenced on the barrier, what was left of her is now covered in sand with only the lower part of one of her masts sticking out of the sand at 45°.

COLLINGDOC ⑨

(ex *D.B. Hanna*) 1,780 ton Great Lake Steamer built in Hill-on-Tees, Ontario in 1925 and sunk on 28th March 1942. Acquired by the British Admiralty at the same time as the other Great Lakes ship, the *Soriano*. She was partly scrapped by Metal Industries, but sadly over the last fifteen years, the build up of sand to the seaward side of the barrier, has shifted the tide line over 90m (300ft) away from the barrier. The *Collingdoc's* remaining concrete bridge is now surrounded by a sea of grass and likely to disappear forever!

GONDOLIER ⑦

173 ton West Highland Paddle Steamer, built in Glasgow in 1866 and sunk on 21st March 1940. She worked as a passenger ferry for Caledonian MacBrayne on the Caledonian Canal for over 70 years and was acquired by the Admiralty in 1939, her engines, boiler, sponsons, paddle-boxes and saloons were removed in Inverness and the hulk was towed to Scapa Flow. Sadly she rolled over, drifted off and sank in deep water during a gale. She is now buried in the sand somewhere east of Barrier IV.

The Pontos before the rising sand finally covered her

JUNIATA ⑤

(ex *Sprucol*) 1,139 ton twin-screw motor tanker, built in Sunderland in 1918, registered in London and sunk on 17th April 1940. The Juniata was later removed and ran aground in Inganess Bay. Wrongly identified as the Vordefjell, the Juniata sits upright out of the water and makes for easy snorkelling.

The Juniata at Inganess Bay

MADJA ⑧

This was a concrete barge, formerly owned by James Anderson of Stromness and was sunk north of *Clio I* on 28th February 1939. Again, nothing remains of this barge, in fact it does not appear on any subsequent plans made after the barriers were in place. It is to be assumed that she was salvaged, scrapped and any remains are now lost under the sand.

The Collingdoc is now over 100 metres from the sea and liable to disappear forever

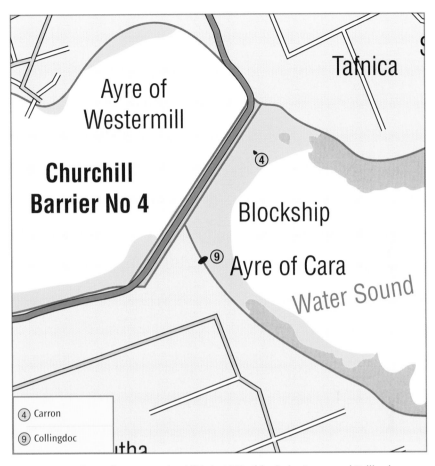

Only small parts remain visible in 2005 of both the Carron and Collingdoc

Barrier 4 shortly after completion

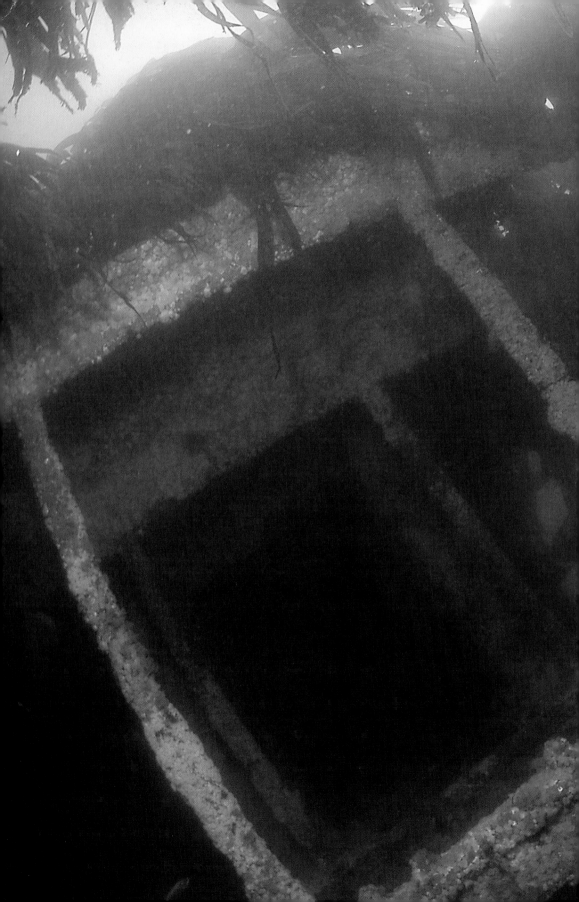

BLOCKSHIP BARRIER 5: BURRA SOUND

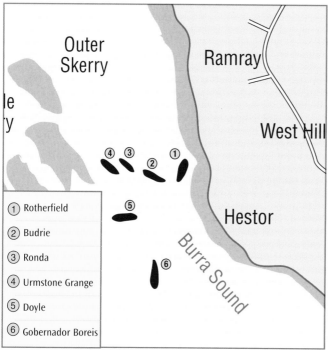

Outer
Skerry

le
'y

Ramray

West Hill

④ ③
② ①

⑤

Hestor

①	Rotherfield
②	Budrie
③	Ronda
④	Urmstone Grange
⑤	Doyle
⑥	Gobernador Boreis

⑥

Burra Sound

Blockships sunk during World War I

WORLD WAR I BLOCKSHIPS

Burra Sound is by far the most exciting of all the Blockship areas, as it was decided that it would be too costly to bridge the gap between Hestor on Graemsay and Burraquoy on Hoy. Unfortunately the wreck of the *Inverlane* finally succumbed to the punishing tides and collapsed after a series of particularly bad winter storms. The wreck always stemmed part of the tidal flow for so long that dive boats were able to moor alongside her and wait for the optimum times to dive the other three more intact Blockships. The remains of the more prominent shallow wrecks of the *Urmstone Grange; Budrie; Rotherfeld* and the *Ronda* were all dispersed in the 1960's by a team of Royal Engineers and these wreckage parts now lie scattered amidst the Middle and Outer Skerries and opposite Windywalls and Ramray on the Island of Graemsay. Really no-one dives on these remains anymore as the parts are all in quite shallow water, covered in a thick growth of kelp and are, of course, still subject to the strength of the tidal race as it sweeps in and out of Scapa Flow each day. Although divers still visit the remains of the *Inverlane* occasionally, or by accident! almost everyone dives only on the *Doyle; Gobernador Boreis* and the *Tabarka;* these three blockships are regarded as their most favourite dives by many visitors to Scapa Flow.

BUDRIE ②

(ex *Cannig*; ex *Golconda*) 2,252 ton steamer, 86.9m (285ft) long, built in Glasgow in 1882, registered in Bombay and sunk on 3rd October 1915. Concrete ballasted, she stayed in position pointing in a westerly direction and was second in place, to the west of the *Rotherfeld*. She finally collapsed and some of her parts were swept out to sea. The *Inverlane* was sunk on top of her and parts of the *Budrie* are still under the hull plates of the remains of the *Inverlane*.

DOYLE ⑤

⊗ **Location:** Lying across the current, south of the *Tabarka* on the inside of Burra Sound.

◉ **Depth:** 13-17m (42-56ft).

◉ **Conditions:** Wreck is quite open with a spectacular mid section for penetration.

① **Special Considerations:**

The tidal stream here is punishing to say the least and whilst this is a slack water dive, invariably it ends as a drift dive.

→ **Access:** By boat only and then only on the boat captain's command.

◓ **Skill Level:** Beginner to Intermediate, but some wreck diving experience is preferable.

(ex *Widdrington*) The *Doyle* was a single screw coastal steamer built in Troon, Ayrshire and weighed 1,761 tons. At 79.3m (260ft) long, she was requisitioned by the Admiralty and sunk on 7th October 1914. The early attempts at sinking the Blockships were rather hit or miss and in the *Doyle's* case, it was a miss. The engineers did not take into account the speed at which the tide changes and as the ship was unballasted when she started to go under, she drifted off station into the interior of Burra Sound and now lies directly across the tidal race. She was deemed useless as a Blockship, but from my personal opinion is now quite possibly the best dive in Scapa Flow.

The *Doyle* is the smallest of the three accessible Blockships and is instantly recognizable by her intact curved bows and stern. Lying on her port side, the more exposed starboard hull is covered in dwarf plumose anemones *(Metridium senile)*, seaweeds and sponges. Her

wooden decking has all rotted away, but virtually all of her ribs, posts and lower sections of masts are still in place allowing divers many safe access points into the interior of the ship at various levels. The ship is still robust enough to allow for full safe and easy access and the interior allows you to extend your dive into the time when the current starts to run once more. Hull plates have come away over the years and the light now streams in through a huge number of square holes making for a rather superb cathedral-like quality. Ballan wrasse, cuckoo wrasse and conger eels are found in the interior and huge schools of juvenile saithe and Pollack swirl around the superstructure. The stern is also largely intact, topped with kelp and the huge blades of her single propeller are covered in anemones and small pincushion sea urchins. Once slack water passes, divers are recommended to just drift away from the wreck as you will only pull down the dive boat's shotline. Divers should deploy a delayed surface marker buoy and the dive boat will follow your easy progress into Burra Sound and be there to collect you.

There has been some confusion in the past over the *Doyle* and the *Moyle*. My good friend Ian Whittaker who compiled the excellent wreck resource book 'Off Scotland' finally solved the problem. The *Doyle's* sister ship *Moyle*, identical in size and weight and had several owners. She was purchased by the Admiralty in 1940 as a 'Special Services Vessel'; and was actually also sunk as a blockship, but this time in Dunkirk on 4th June 1940.

Internal/external views of The Doyle

GOBERNADOR BOREIS ⑥
(EX WORDSWORTH)

(X) **Location:** The most southerly of the Burra Sound
Blockships, it lies southeast of the *Doyle*.

(⌖) **Depth:** 13-17m (42-56ft).

(⌖) **Conditions:** Generally clear water, but ship is
completely open with
recognizable parts throughout.

(!) **Special Considerations:**
Always done at slack water on an
incoming tide, divers will usually
complete their dive in open water
current.

(→) **Access:** By boat only and then only on the
Captain's instructions.

(⊙) **Skill Level:** Beginner to Intermediate, but some
wreck diving experience is preferable.

The *Gobernador Boreis* was a 2,332 ton single
screw steamer, 87.2m (286ft) long and built in
West Hartlepool in 1882. She worked as a
whaling ship and cargo steamer, in Chile,
Argentina, and the Falkland Islands for many
years but had been pretty well abandoned
before the British Admiralty acquired the hulk
and had her towed all the way to Scapa Flow.
She was another of the early naval mistakes, as
she behaved exactly the same as the *Doyle*,
having failed to sink on time; she drifted into
Burra Sound before sinking in a depth too deep
for her to be an effective Blockship on 12th
October 1914.

The *Goby* as she is affectionately known
predominantly lies on her port side, but the
hull has twisted over the years and her stern
angles to starboard. Another very robust
steamship, her bows, midships and stern are all
relatively intact. Both the interior of the bows
and stern are covered in dwarf plumose
anemones and the outer hull casing is topped
with kelp. The decks are gone inside the stern
as well as her portholes, but the strengthening
ribs and pillars are still strong and covered in
marine life. Under the open stern, her rudder

Stern view of the Gobernador Boreis

and huge propeller are also intact and divers
can easily explore the area out of the current.

The *Goby* is pretty well broken up and a lot of
divers enjoy her mid section where the boilers
and huge pistons are located, but perhaps the
most striking aspect is the openness of the ship.
The metal ribs and spars are covered in marine
life and divers are always accompanied by
ballan wrasse (*Labrus bergylta*). You can gain
entry into the lower parts of the ship, but these
are not as interesting or as scenic as on the
Doyle. Part of the starboard hull plate has
fallen in and created a swimthrough towards

the boilers, behind these is the massive block of the steam engine with her huge pistons, rods and crankshaft visible inside. Schools of fish have made their home on the wreck and much of the metal areas are smothered in anemones, sea squirts and pincushion starfish.

Note: Due to her position in relation to the other Blockships in Burra Sound and located further into the sound, divers can enjoy a little extra time on her at slack water with a slightly less ferocity of current. Keep an eye on the kelp when you are inside the protected areas of the wreck, as it is a great indicator of which way the current is running and how strong it will be when you leave the ship's protective embrace for an easy drift into Burra Sound.

Internal views of the Gobernador Boreis

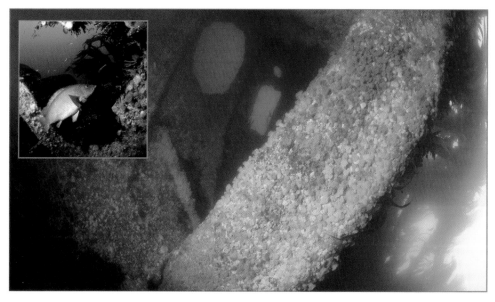

RONDA ③

The Rotherfield & The Budrie shortly after their sinking

(ex *Rydal Holme*) 1,941 ton steel, single screw steamer, 83.5m (274ft) long, built in Sunderland in 1889, registered in Hull and sunk on 20th August 1915. Not wanting to make the same mistake with this sinking, the *Ronda* was concrete ballasted and she lay where she was sunk, pointing in a southeasterly direction. Her position slightly overlapped that of the *Urmstone Grange* the last ship sunk to the west of Burra Sound. Deemed a navigation hazard after the war, she was finally blown up and dispersed in 1962. Large chunks of her washed out to sea, but some larger parts can still be found covered in kelp on the Hoy Skerries.

ROTHERFIELD ①

2,831 ton single screw steamer, 97.5m (320ft) long, built in West Hartlepool in 1889 and registered in London, sunk on 23rd September 1914. The most easterly of the Blockships sunk in Burra Sound, her stern was tilted up in quite shallow water for many years and her bows pointed almost due south, hard against the shore. Quite distinctive for many years, she

finally collapsed and became a navigational hazard, as the *Inverlane* was still so prominent at the time. Naval engineers blew her apart in 1962, her remains are now covered in kelp in very shallow water.

URMSTONE GRANGE ④

3,423 ton single screw coastal freighter, 103.6m (340ft) long built in Belfast in 1894, registered in London, she was the first of the Blockships to be sunk at Burra Sound on 22nd September 1914. The most westerly of the Burra Sound Blockships, she had quietly collapsed over the years, creating a navigational hazard to all shipping. Like the *Rotherfeld* and the *Budrie*, she was blown apart and dispersed in 1962. Larger parts are now mixed in with the *Budrie*, covered in kelp and found nearby on the shallow Hoy Skerries.

Photographs Courtesy of Andy Cuthbertson

Archive photograph of the Urmstone Grange

WORLD WAR II BLOCKSHIPS

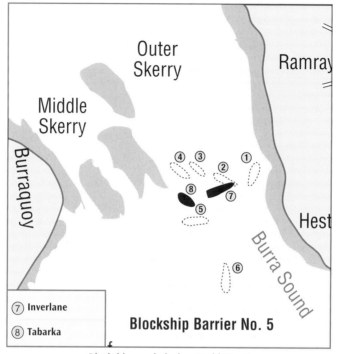

Blockships sunk during World War II

Archive photograph of the Inverlane before the relentless tidal race and winter storms dispersed the wreck over a wide area

INVERLANE ⑦

⊗ Location: Lying across the current, east of the *Tabarka* on the inside of Burra Sound.

◉ Depth: 13-17m (42-56ft).

◉ Conditions: Wreck is now completely ripped apart, only her bows remain relatively intact in shallower water.

① Special Considerations:
The tidal stream here is punishing to say the least and whilst this is a slack water dive, invariably it ends as a drift dive.

➔ Access: By boat only and then only on the boat captain's command.

◉ Skill Level: Beginner to Intermediate, but some wreck diving experience is preferable.

The *Inverlane* was originally an 8,900 ton tanker built in Vegesack, Germany and registered in

Above and overleaf: Interior views of the Inverlane

Dublin. She was one of seven owned by the Inver Tanker company. She was mined in the North Sea by the very nation who had built her and her stern was removed and attached to another ship under construction at the time. She was then mined a second time and lost off South Shields in 1939. The forward section weighing 9,141 tons was sealed amidships and towed to Burra Sound where she was sunk on top of the site of the *Budrie* on 30th May 1944.

For many years the *Inverlane* was the jewel in the crown of Scapa Flow and was highly regarded as one of the ultimate wreck dives in Europe, the forward section of the bows were high and dry and the local dive boats used to moor onto the hulk at any state of tide. Thereafter, divers clambered aboard the ship, kitted up and made access through several of the open hatchways into the interior of the ship. Once inside the ship, divers could enjoy the site completely sheltered from any current. The interior was completely open and a couple of friendly seals would scare the bubbles out of you when they snuck up behind you. The gaping end of the hulk was really quite something and when you got the currents right at slack water, you could swim over to the *Tabarka*. Sadly the merciless tidal race finally took its toll; the *Inverlane* healed over to starboard and precariously hung on for a few months before it finally collapsed. The hull is now flattened and is spread over a wide area, covered in kelp, it is easy to miss and only rarely visited. The bows are still relatively intact and still quite clean of encrusting marine life, but even this is nearing collapse and it will probably go quite quickly.

TABARKA ⑧

(X) **Location:** Lying west of the *Inverlane's* former position and north of the *Doyle*.

(≈) **Depth:** 14-18m (47-60ft).

(≈) **Conditions:** Made at slack water and the dive is undertaken inside the upturned hull.

(!) **Special Considerations:**

As mentioned, this dive is made inside the upturned hull, but there are ample entry and exit points, care should be taken amongst the steel beams covered in marine life.

(→) **Access:** Can be done as a shore dive, but more common by boat.

(≈) **Skill Level:** Beginner to Intermediate, but some wreck diving experience is preferable.

(ex *Pollux*) The *Tabarka* was built in Rotterdam in 1909 and seized by the British Admiralty off Falmouth in 1940. Fairly robust at 2,642tons, this steel, single screw steamer was sailed under her own steam to Scapa Flow and originally sunk at Barrier I on 23rd March 1941. With the obvious success of the ongoing construction of the Churchill Barriers, it was decided to refloat the *Tabarka* move her to Burra Sound and sink her as an additional Blockship, now that this was the only major entrance in the western approaches which could have access to enemy shipping traffic. She was subsequently refloated in 1944, moved and sunk in Burra Sound on 27th July 1944.

One would think that the Naval Engineers and Metal Industries would have got it right by now, as this was one of the last Blockships to be sunk. Again, the sinking process did not go

well and the ship turned turtle, her ballast shifting and drifted into the sound before sinking near the aft section of the *Inverlane*. Now completely upside down, but with numerous access points, she is one of the favourite wreck dives for divers visiting Scapa Flow.

The dive is undertaken inside the wreck and divers can explore the ship through various levels in her interior as all of the wooden decking has rotted away. Her three boilers are amidships but there is still plenty of room to move over them to the bows or the stern. The stern is more open with numerous access points through the deteriorating hull and the interior has been likened to a giant diving playground. All of her interior metal areas are covered in anemones, dead men's fingers and sea squirts. There is plenty to see for everyone

Above and overleaf: Interior views of the Tabarka

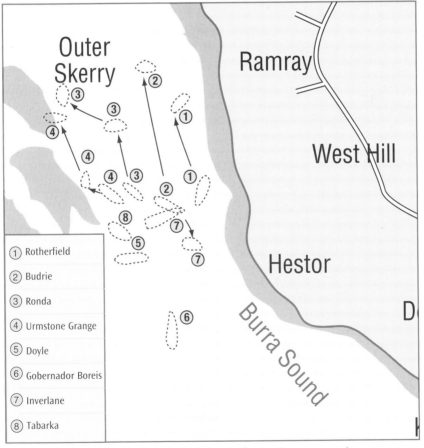

Position of wrecks in 2005 clearly showing distances moved

MAINLAND

Bremse Site

Orphir Bay ❶

Bayern Turret Site

Brummer

Cöln II

Karlsruhe II

Kronprinz Wilhelm

Markgraf

Barrel of Butter ❷

Kaiser Site

König

Dresden II

S36

CAVA

Coal Barge

Seydlitz Site

V83

Von Der Tann Site

V78

Vanguard

RYSA LITTLE

Gutter Sound ❸

West Weddell Sound ❹

Prudentia

Concrete Barge

Nevi Skerry ❼

F2

YC21

FARA

B109

Mara

UB116

HMS Strathgarry

Rose Valley

FLOTTA

S54

Hoxa Head ❽

HOY

Roedean

Kirk Bay ❺

Stanger Head ❻

James Barrie

SWITHA ❾

SOUTH WALLS

1   0   1   2   3   4 Kilometres

Scale

Conger Eel

Scapa Flow Reef Dives

SCAPA FLOW REEF DIVES (MUCH MORE THAN METAL!)

Undoubtedly, the lion's share of all diving done in Scapa Flow goes to the various deteriorating shipwrecks, however, for those local divers in the know and for those visiting divers who want to see another aspect of Scapa Flow, then there is a selection of reef dives which give a wide range of habitats and variety of marine life which is surprisingly indicative of the Scottish west coast sea lochs.

Sadly, much of the shore line around Scapa Flow is unreachable by road and when a road does drop near the water's edge, the seabed is generally shallow, tidal and rather silty, but for one exception at Orphir Bay. All of the other reef dives mentioned here are only accessible by boat, however all of them are superb and really, it should take little coaxing to visit these sites, as most are conveniently located nearby a historic wreck, which are usually visited by one or other of the Scapa Flow dive boats when they are within the vicinity. Consider the island of Flotta, rarely visited but for the remains of the German Motor Torpedo Boat *S-54*, however there are four superb dive sites in the immediate area, offering spectacular walls, masses of marine life and even playful seals.

We expect divers to concentrate on the shipwrecks as the history, myth and mystique surrounding the sinking of these once proud ships is enough to lure anyone to explore them underwater, yet they are all colonized by fascinating marine life which is often overlooked in the search for new and tantalizing bits of scrap. The reefs and shoals of Scapa Flow are amongst some of the best in northern Scotland and should be permitted a fair share of your attention.

SCAPA FLOW MARINE LIFE

The types of marine life that you will find are a curious mixture of the typical Scottish west coast sea lochs combined with North Sea species. Therefore apart from the three species of kelp and countless algaes, we can find wolf fish; at least four species of wrasse; lumpsuckers; suckerfish; thousands of juvenile cod, haddock, herring and saithe; anglerfish; sand eels; skate; dogfish; dahlia and plumose anemones; pincushion starfish; long-clawed squat lobsters; brittlestars; featherstars; tunicates; hydroids; dead men's fingers; jewel anemones; Devonshire cup corals and even the Scottish coral, maerle.

ORPHIR BAY ①

Descending down over the kelp

(X) **Location:** Turn off the A964 Orphir Road at Midland and proceed towards the Earl's Church. There is a public right of way down to the shore, but you must remember to close the farm gates if the farmer has livestock in the fields. Nearby the site of the salvaged Light Cruiser *Bremse*.

Depth: 6-12m (20-40ft)

Conditions: No current, this site makes a great night dive.

(!) **Special Considerations:**
Best at full tide as it is a treacherous walk over the slippery rocks to the water's edge.

(→) **Access:** Directly off the shore to either side of the wedge shaped rocky reef that cuts the bay in half.

Diver experience:
All levels of diver.

Friendly cuckoo wrasse are common

The large rock finger in the middle of the bay gets exposed at low tide and is topped with kelp, fucus and other algae. To the east, the seabed slopes gently from gravel to fine sand and on the west of the reef; it is of a finer silt sediment. Both parts of the bay slope gently to 12m (40ft), then more rapidly to 25m (80ft). Known as a shore dive training site and as an excellent night diving location, divers can find lots of shrimp; juvenile flounders; gobies and numerous wrasse. On the cleaner sand peacock worms and burrowing anemones are common.

Entelurus Aequorus Snake Pipefish

BARREL OF BUTTER ②

(X) **Location:** Central Scapa Flow, close by all of the sunken German Fleet.

(👁) **Depth:** 12-30m (40-100ft)

(👁) **Conditions:** Visibility can be reduced around this area.

(!) **Special Considerations:**
Try not to make too much of a splash when you enter the water, as you may chase away some of the seals.

(→) **Access:** By boat only and dependent on the wind, this will alter the dive profile, but most divers will either circumnavigate the rocks or dive deep to look for scallops!

(🕐) **Diver experience:**
Suitable for all levels of diver.

An angler fish poses on the boulders

Dead Mens' Fingers cover the rocks

The Barrel of Butter is a large rocky reef that juts up out of the middle of Scapa Flow and is visible due to the large navigation tower which sits prominently on the top. It is around the western approaches to Barrel of Butter that all of the German Fleet are arranged. The dive consists of a large boulder slope with drops down to 30m (100ft). On the boulders can be found ascidian sea-squirts; feather starfish; plumose anemones; dead men's fingers; and long-clawed squat lobsters. There are always lots of wrasse to be found here as well as numerous juvenile haddock. The seabed is a mix of fine sand, gravel and silty mud and has all of the associated species that you would expect such as scallops; queen scallops; anglerfish; luidia starfish; horse mussels and burrowing anemones.

Seal at The Barrel of Butter

GUTTER SOUND (RUMMAGE DIVE) ③

(X) **Location:** In the channel between Lyness on the Island of Hoy and the western shores of Fara. Nearby the wrecks *F2; YC21* and the *MV Mara*.

(☻) **Depth:** 16-19m (54-63ft).

(☻) **Conditions:** Often a gentle current flowing through the sound, but the seabed can be silty.

(!) **Special Considerations:**
Keep well clear of the fish farm to the west of Fara as the dive boats may have difficulty in retrieving you if you stray too close.

(→) **Access:** By boat only.

(☻) **Diver experience:**
Suitable for all levels of diver.

Circular Crabs enjoy the mud and shell debris seabed

Queen scallops are very common on this site

This site is often done after the dive boats have visited either the *F2* and *YC21* or the *MV Mara* wrecks. Lunch is generally moored up at Lyness for divers to visit the Scapa Flow Visitor centre. This afternoon dive is seen as a general rummage around to look for old bottles, scallops, crockery and other flotsam and jetsam left over from the anchored German and British Fleets over the last 100 years or so. Large amounts of coal can be found as well as stone jars. All of these recovered items should of course be presented to the Receiver of Wreck or gifted to the Stromness Museum. Marine life in the flat seabed of the sound includes scallops; queen scallops; dog whelks; blennies; edible crabs; circular crabs; horse mussels and the ubiquitous wrasse.

Edible crabs are everywhere

WEST WEDDELL SOUND ④

ⓧ Location: Between the south eastern shore of Fara and the north western shore of Flotta. Nearby the wreck of the *Prudentia*.

☺ Depth: 14-16m (46-54ft)

☺ Conditions: This is generally done as a drift dive usually on the incoming tide when the water is clearer.

① Special Considerations: Divers should be careful of boat traffic as the ferry service between the southern islands all pass through Weddel Sound.

→ Access: Usually by boat, but can be accessed from the pier to the south of Sutherland.

☺ Diver experience: Suitable for all levels of diver.

Suckerfish and sea urchin on Maerle

This is one of the few sites within the region of Scapa Flow where the Scottish coral, maerle can be found. This curious stony bryozoan is not actually a true coral, but the pink colour makes for a rather colourful dive as many different species of marine life can also be found in its midst. Small shrimps; ghost crabs; velvet swimming crabs; hydroids; suckerfish; sea urchins; wrasse; gobies; peacock worms and scallops can be found. Large boulders are covered in dead men's fingers and thousands of brittle starfish can also be found around huge dahlia anemones. This is a great dive when you get the tides right as the gentle current lets you cover a huge distance with very little effort.

Dahlia anenomes are very colourful on this site

The rare Yarrell's Blenny can also be found here

KIRK BAY ⑤

⊗ **Location:** The large 'U' shaped bay to the south of Flotta. Close to the wrecks of the *S54; UB116; HMS Strathgarry* and the *MV James Barrie*.

⊚ **Depth:** 15-30m (50-100ft)

⊚ **Conditions:** Sheltered from northerly winds, but it can be very choppy when the wind is from the southeast.

① **Special Considerations:**
Divers should be aware of the sometimes very strong current which sweeps along the south coast of Flotta as the incoming tide floods into Scapa Flow.

→ **Access:** Usually by boat, as the cliff side is quite steep and rarely negotiated by shore divers.

◔ **Diver experience:**
Suitable for all levels of diver.

Luidia Starfish can be found eating the brittlestars at this location

This is actually quite a good drift dive, but divers should be aware of the strength of the current as they approach either Cave of Banks to the west or House Geo and Stanger Head to the east. There are lots of kelp covered boulders in the shallows and numerous swimming and edible crabs can be found as well as lobsters and squat lobsters. Flounders; turbot and even skate are commonly seen here as well as burrowing sea urchins; tube anemones and simply huge plumose anemones and dahlia anemones as you reach the 30m (100ft) mark. This area is synonymous with huge brittlestar beds which cover mounds of dead maerle which has been swept round from Weddel Sound.

Large Plumose Anemone are found in deep water

STANGER HEAD ⑥

Ⓧ Location: The south easterly point of Flotta, conveniently located nearby the wrecks of the *S54; UB116; HMS Strathgarry* and the *MV James Barrie*.

Depth: 15-30m (50-100ft)

Conditions: Easy dive down a cliff and boulder face, site is exposed to southerly gales.

Special Considerations:

! The current around Stanger Head can be quite severe on the incoming tide, and it is best not to venture further than the two prominent sea stacks (Known as the Old Man and Old Woman of Flotta).

Access: By boat only. The dive boats will drop divers off just next to the sea stacks where there is a sheltered cove.

Diver experience:
Suitable for all levels of diver.

This is a dive down a rock and boulder slope covered in dead men's fingers, sea squirts and feather starfish. Where the boulders meet the wall, numerous cuckoo wrasse; goldsinny; ling; octopus and blennies can be found. The area is also well known for nudibranch spotting. As the boulders meet the gravel and sand seabed, this quickly makes way to bedrock ridges which slope down into the sound where squat lobsters; brittle starfish; scallops; octopus and hydroids can be found. This site is one of several monitored every six months by Talisman Oil Company from the oil terminal on Flotta to check for any environmental impact. This is a superb dive site and should not be missed.

The Sea Stacks Old man & Woman of Flotta

A diver on the cliff wall at Stanger Head

Ballan Wrasse are common on this site

NEVI SKERRY ⑦

⊗ **Location:** West of the north westerly tip of Flotta, the Skerry is marked by a navigation light. Close to the wrecks of the *S54; UB116; HMS Strathgarry* and the *MV James Barrie.*

◉ **Depth:** 20-25m (66-80ft)

◉ **Conditions:** Current is to be expected around the Skerry and care should be taken.

⚠ **Special Considerations:**
Keep clear of the bottom as there are large pressure ridges of sand and gravel which get stirred up when the tide is running.

➔ **Access:** By boat only, and then only when conditions are near perfect.

◔ **Diver experience:**
Suitable for intermediate to advanced divers.

Colourful Cuckoo Wrasse show their colours in the summer

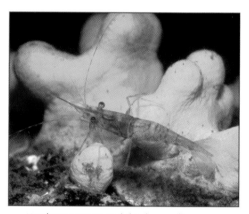

Northern Prawns and dead mens fingers are common to the site

Spiny starfish are more prevalent on the deeper boulders

The rapidly dropping bedrock quickly makes way to huge boulders which are all covered in kelp. Coarse clean sand can be found at the bottom of the boulder slope at 24m (77ft) which gradually becomes finer as you descend deeper. Bits of wreckage can be found all around the site, testimony to the numbers of ships which have struck the rock and in particular many naval ships which were subsequently repaired by Metal Industries during WWII. Mermaid's purses from common skate are often found, as are dogfish; wrasse; squat lobsters; sea-squirts; queen scallops and hydroids. The large pressure ridges of sand and gravel are quite interesting to see as they are created by the strong tidal movements, particularly during spring tides.

HOXA HEAD ⑧

(X) **Location:** The most north westerly point of
South Ronaldsay, very convenient
when trying to dive the wreck of the
James Barrie or the *Strathgarry*.

(👀) **Depth:** 9-30m (30-100ft)

(🌊) **Conditions:** Quite exposed on the corner and some
current is to be expected.

(!) **Special Considerations:**
Some of the swimthroughs under the
boulders are quite narrow, so care
should be taken in case you get stuck!

(→) **Access:** By boat only.

(🧭) **Diver experience:**
Suitable for all levels of diver.

*Long clawed squat lobsters enjoy the boulder and
rocky slope*

Hoxa Head is often dived when the currents on
the *James Barrie* just never let up. However it is
a great dive in its own right and should not be
overlooked. There are some huge (house-sized)
boulders all jumbled together to create
interesting gullies, canyons and swimthroughs.
Topped with kelp, their sides are covered in
dead men's fingers and plumose anemones.
Sea-squirts; scorpion fish and wrasse are
everywhere and as you reach the gravel seabed
at 28m (94ft), small anemones; common
starfish; brittle starfish; queen scallops and
large horse mussels can be found. I even found
a baby octopus hiding in an empty mussel
shell.

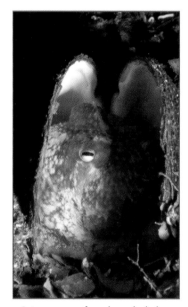

Octopuses are found regularly here

Scorpion fish pose for the photographer

SWITHA ⑨

(X) **Location:** North Shore of the Island of Switha, south of Flotta. Close to the wrecks of the *S54; UB116; HMS Strathgarry* and the *MV James Barrie*.

(👁) **Depth:** 18m (60ft)

(🌀) **Conditions:** Quite sheltered from most weather.

(!) **Special Considerations:**
Divers should be aware of the strong tidal streams as you approach the corner at North Taing, so it is often better to dive to the southwest and is easier for the pick-up by the dive boat.

(→) **Access:** By Boat only.

(🕐) **Diver experience:**
Suitable for all levels of diver.

Pincushion Starfish thrive in these conditions

The north coast of Switha is rarely dived, due to the heady excesses of so many other great reefs and wrecks, however should you decide to venture outside Scapa Flow, then this is a great drift dive along huge slabs of rock which overlay loose patches of sand and gravel. There are always tons of fish including pollack; haddock; saithe and wrasse. Peacock worms; sea-squirts and feather starfish can be found on the slopes. This is a very brightly lit site with generally fairly clear water, hence the kelp forest can be found down to 18m (60ft).

Common sea urchins graze the algae

Deep water dahlia anemone are found in the seabed from 18m

Right: Long clawed squat lobsters can be found on the Barrel of Butter

Appendix

ORKNEY DIVE BOAT OPERATORS ASSOCIATION

Halton Charters

3 Ness Road, Stromness, Orkney. KW16 3DL

Tel: (01856) 851532; fax: (0870) 0516 364

E-mail: bob@mvhalton.co.uk

Web: http://www.mvhalton.co.uk

Orkney Islands Charters

Northolme, Dounby, Orkney. KW17 2JB

Tel: (01856) 771314

E-mail: mervyn@orkneyislandscharters.co.uk

Web: http://www.orkneyislandscharters.co.uk

Roving Eye Enterprises

Westrow Lodge, Orphir, Orkney. KW17 2RD

Tel: (01856) 811309; Fax: (01856) 811737

E-mail: k2bichan@aol.com

Web: http://www.rovingeye.co.uk

Scapa Scuba

Lifeboat House, 13 Ness Road, Stromness, Orkney. KW16 3DL

Tel/Fax: (01856) 851218

E-Mail: diving@scapascuba.co.uk

Web: www.scapascuba.co.uk

Scapa Flow Charters

5 Church Road, Stromness, Orkney. KW16 3BA

Tel/Fax: (01856) 850879

E-mail: enquiry@jeanelaine.co.uk

Web: http://www.jeanelaine.co.uk

Scapa Flow Diving Centre

Cara 3, Grimness, South Ronaldsay, Orkney. KW17 2TH

Tel: (01856) 831821

E-mail: dave.scapaflowdivingcentre@virgin.net

Web: http://www.scapaflowdivingcentre.com

Scapa Flow Technical

Polrudden, Peerie Sea Loan, Kirkwall, Orkney. KW15 1UH

Tel: (01856) 874761 or Tel: (01856) 870950

E-mail: john@scapaflow.com

Web: http://www.scapaflow.com

Valkyrie

Northcroft Partnership

Northfield, Holm,

Orkney. KW17 2RZ

E-mail: hazel@mv-valkyrie.co.uk

Web: http://www.valkyrie.co.uk

Stromness Diving Centre

Barkland, Carlston Drive, Stromness, Orkney. KW16 3JL

Tel/Fax: (01856) 850624

E-mail: steve@triton.force9.co.uk

Web: http://www.orknet.co.uk/scapa/triton.htm

Sunrise Charters

Carradale, Weyland Bay, Kirkwall, Orkney. KW15 1TD

Tel: (01856) 874425; Fax: (01856) 874725

E-mail: dougie@sunrisecharters.co.uk

Web: http://www.sunrisecharters.co.uk

The Diving Cellar

4 Victoria Street, Stromness, Orkney. KW16 3AA

Tel: (01856) 850055; Tel/Fax: (01856) 850395

E-mail: leigh@divescapaflow.co.uk

Web: http://www.divescapaflow.co.uk

Scapa Flow dive boats moored up in Stromness Harbour

ORKNEY DIVE BOAT OPERATORS' ASSOCIATION (ODBOA) CODE OF PRACTICE

General Responsibilities

Dive boat skippers are responsible for safety of all passengers and crew while on board their vessel.

Dive boat owners are responsible for ensuring both vessels and skipper have appropriate certification for area of operation and that certificates and training records are in place

Divers are responsible for the possession of a current diving qualification appropriate to the planned dive and a valid certificate of medical fitness to dive.

Diving operations are the responsibility of the diving group, individual or nominated diving supervisor. Divers are responsible for discussing dive plans with the skipper through a nominated representative.

The skipper may advise on matters considered relevant to the dive (e.g. changes in sea condition, surface visibility, tides). If necessary, the skipper has the authority to terminate the dive or suggest an alternative if considered unsafe or sea/weather conditions are considered unsuitable.

Vessel owners are responsible for ensuring any equipment used in provision of a diving service (e.g. compressor) is suitable and that maintenance, test certificates and training records are in date.

Insurance

Dive boat owners will ensure that the vessel has valid Passenger and Third Party Liability Insurance.

The dive boat is only insured for divers whilst they are onboard. Divers are responsible for ensuring that they have adequate insurance cover for their diving activities.

Vessel Communications

All dive boats will carry adequate and working communications equipment including VHF and keep a listening watch on Channel 16 and any other agreed working VHF Channel.

Dive boats will establish and maintain communication with any vessel(s) already on the dive site, identify current situation and agree diving/vessel manoeuvre procedures to be followed.

Dive boats to display correct dive signals (A-Flag) when divers are in the water. Signals to be removed when vessel not involved in diving operation.

All vessels to proceed at a safe speed in areas where divers are in-water.

A watch will be kept at all times when in the vicinity of a dive site for surfacing divers and divers on surface. This should be particularly observed when putting engine into gear.

A safe distance will be maintained from the shot while the boat is on standby, bearing in mind both keeping clear of surfacing divers and a need to keep watch for divers and any other vessel traffic.

Diver Location

When diving in tidal locations or in recognized navigation channels away from known wrecks sites and shot lines, divers will carry surface marker buoys (SMB's) or decompression bags. This is particularly important when undertaking long periods of in-water decompression.

The diver is responsible for informing the skipper of any intention to move away from the wreck and/or shot line and planned dive durations.

The skipper is responsible for informing the divers of any known hazards (e.g. navigation lanes and ferry routes). Divers are responsible for planning dives accordingly.

The skipper will communicate with OIC Operations Room at Scapa before diving the wreck of the 'Strathgarry' in Hoxa Sound.

Emergencies

Dive boat skippers are responsible for coordinating emergency procedures onboard the vessel and complying with agreed emergency communication channels. In the event of an emergency involving a diving incident, HM Coastguard should be immediately notified on Channel 16.

Dive boat skippers will maintain a log of contact details and next of kin for all passengers on board.

Divers are responsible for keeping adequate logs of their dives to assist in the event of a diving incident.

Other dive boats in the area will remain on standby in the event of an emergency including a diving incident and assist where necessary.

Dive boat owners are responsible for ensuring all vessels carry a means of recovering casualties from the water and that the dive boat skippers are familiar in techniques of retrieval of an injured or unconscious diver from the water.

Dive boat owners are responsible for ensuring all vessels carry O2 administration equipment and that this is maintained as appropriate. Dive boat skippers will be trained in the use of O2 administration equipment.

Wreck Protection

ODBOA supports the national Respect our Wrecks Code of Practice and recognizes the Orkney Voluntary Underwater Conservation Zone.

Due to the protected status of the German High Seas Fleet under the Ancient Monumenmts and Archaeological Areas Act 1979, divers may not carry crowbars or salvage equipment when diving the wrecks of the Cöln, Brummer, Dresden, Markgraf, Konig, Kronprinz Wilhelm and Karlsruhe.

ODBOA supports the location and discovery of new wrecks. Wreck location and recovery of any artifacts must be undertaken within the law and reported to the Receiver of Wreck. It is the responsibility of the individual divers to undertake all reporting and measures necessary under the law.

HMS Royal Oak, HMS Vanguard and HMS Hampshire are recognized War Graves and as such are proposed as controlled wrecks under the Protection of Military Remains Act 1986. Diving is not permitted without a valid licence, and skippers will not allow diving on these wrecks without the possession of such a licence. No crowbars or other salvage equipment may be carried.

Orkney Dive Boat Operators Association

Code of Practice – Revision 1.1

COP October 2001 Page 1 of 1

Web page 22 March 2004. ©ODBOA

ORKNEY DIVE BOATS

Virtually all of the dive boats are converted motor fishing vessels. All are able to offer air, oxygen and nitrox to any percentage, to suit your diving capabilities and your equipment's configuration. They are all well serviced with bunks, showers, toilets, kitchen and galley. Entry is by a jump from the side, exit after the dive is up strong sturdy ladders or hydraulic lift.

Valkyrie
Northcroft Partnership
Northfield, Holm, Orkney. KW17 2RZ
Tel: (01856) 781769
E-mail: hazel@mv-valkyrie.co.uk
Web: http://www.valkyrie.co.uk

Crusader
(Scapa Flow Diving Centre)
Tel: (01856) 751492
E-mail: kenny.peace@scapaflowdivingcentre.com
Web: http://www.scapaflowdivingcentre.com

Halton
(Halton Charters)
Tel: (01856) 851532; fax: (0870) 0516 364
E-mail: bob@mvhalton.co.uk
Web: http://www.mvhalton.co.uk

Invincible
(Scapa-Flow)
Tel: (01856) 851110
E-mail: ian@scapa-flow.co.uk
Web: http://www.scapa-flow.co.uk

John L
(The Diving Cellar)
Tel: (01856) 850055; Tel/Fax: (01856) 850395
E-mail: leigh@divescapaflow.co.uk
Web: http://www.divescapaflow.co.uk

Jean Elaine
(Scapa Flow Charters)
Tel/Fax: (01856) 850879
E-mail: enquiry@jeanelaine.co.uk
Web: http://www.jeanelaine.co.uk

Karin
(Scapa Flow)
Tel: (01856) 874761
Mob: 0785 0246831
E-mail: john@scapaflow.com
Web: www.scapaflow.com

Radiant Queen
(Scapa Scuba)
Tel/Fax: (01856) 851218
E-Mail: diving@scapascuba.co.uk
Web: www.scapascuba.co.uk

Sharon Rose
(Scapa Flow Charters)
Tel/Fax: (01856) 850879
E-mail: enquiry@jeanelaine.co.uk
Web: http://www.jeanelaine.co.uk

Sunrise
(Sunrise Charters)
Tel: (01856) 874425; Fax: (01856) 874725
E-mail: dougie@sunrisecharters.co.uk
Web: http://www.sunrisecharters.co.uk

Triton

(Stromness Diving Centre)

Tel/Fax: (01856) 850624

E-mail: steve@triton.force9.co.uk

Web:
http://www.orknet.co.uk/scapa/triton.htm

ALLIED BUSINESSES

Leviathan International (Hard Hat Diving on German Ships & Suit Repairs)

Newdale, Innertown, Stromness. Orkney. KW16 3JP

Tel: (01856) 851002

E-mail: enquiries@leviathan-int.com

Web: http://www.leviathan-int.com

ORKNEY ISLANDS COUNCIL DIVING PERMIT

All visiting divers to Scapa Flow should actually have an authorized Diving Permit endorsed by the Orkney Islands Council, thankfully all of that paperwork is undertaken by members of the Scapa Flow Diving Association. However that does mean that divers must still obey all of the rules in the Permit and take instruction from the skippers from the dive boats as to behaviour and conduct on the various wrecks, as some of them are protected under the Ancient Monuments and Archaeological Areas Act 1979 and Protection of Wrecks Act 1974.

ORKNEY RECOMPRESSION CHAMBER

For many years Scapa Flow had no Recompresion Chamber available for sports divers. There were however two chambers on the islands: one at the hospital in Kirkwall and the other at Flotta Oil terminal. Until the late 90s divers requiring recompression were transferred by air ambulance to the National Hyperbaric Unit at ARI in Aberdeen for treatment. In 1998 a commercial chamber operated at Houton. Between 1999 and 2003 the service was run by NHS Orkney in conjunction with Heriot-Watt University. Now operated by the Orkney Hyperbaric Trust since November 2003, OHT was set up as a non-profit making body to sustain and develop the emergency service. Since the appointment of a permanent chief executive in 2004, NHS Orkney has supported the service through funding for nursing staff and for Stromness practice. The Orkney Unit is a member of the British Hyperbaric Association and a member of the European Baromedical Society.

The Chamber has four qualified staff on call at any time, these are :-

Doctor

Chamber Supervisor

Chamber Support Technician

Chamber Internal Attendant

All of the staff of SULA DIVING are trained in hyperbaric medicine, plus several of the Balfour Hospital's nurses. Boat captains and crew of the Orkney Dive Boat Operators Association are also on call to assist whenever needed. Currently around 18 divers are treated yearly, some purely as a precautionary measure. In fact less divers are being treated now, than ever before. DCS incidents were high a number of years ago but this was principally due to a lack of adequate training in the advanced technologies of Nitrox, Trimix and Rebreathers. Bobby Forbes, the Chamber Supervisor said that the main contributory factor in DCS is dehydration. Divers should be aware of this and keep hydrated at all times. Alcohol, although not necessarily a factor in any DCS incident, should be kept to a minimum during an intense diving week's vacation.

For further information or help, please contact any of the following, depending on the state of emergency or general enquiries.

In an emergency at sea:
Contact Shetland Coastguard on Channel 16

On shore:
Contact Balfour Hospital 01856 888000 You will then be patched through to the Duty Doctor and Duty Officer.

SULA Diving (Scientific Underwater Logistics & Diving) who operate the chamber can be contacted on the following:-

Tel Bobby Forbes on 01856 850285;
Fax 01856 851668

E.Mail: bobby.forbes@sdsc.com

Bibliography & Acknowledgements

Admiralty Hydrographic Department, Taunton: Maps X96-1; X96-2; X96-3; X96-4; X96-5.

Baird, Robert. N.: *Shipwrecks of the North of Scotland*, Birlinn, Edinburgh, 2003.

Bowman, Gerald: *The Man Who Bought A Navy*, George G.Harrap, London 1964.

Brown, M & Meehan, P: *Scapa Flow*, Allen Lane, London, 1968.

Burrows, C.W.: *Scapa and a Camera*, The Orcadian, Orkney, 2007.

Chapel Preservation Committee: *Orkney's Italian Chapel*, Shetland Litho, Lerwick, 2000.

Clouston, J. Storey: *The Spy In Black*, Seabridge, Orkney, 1917, 2007.

Costello, John & Hughes, Terry: *The Battle of the Atlantic*, Fontana/Collins, London, 1977.

Cormack, Alastair & Anne: *Bolsters, Blocks, Barriers*, The Orkney View, Orkney, 1992.

Cousins, Geoffrey: *The Story of Scapa Flow*, Frederick Muller Ltd., 1965.

Cox, E.F.: *Eight Years Salvage Work at Scapa Flow*, 1932.

Die Deutche Flotte 1848-1945, Lohse-Eissing Verlag, Wilhelmshaven, 1962.

Duthie, Johnny: *Lest We Forget Daisy*, The Orcadian.

Ferguson, David S.: *Shipwrecks of Hoy Sound*, Herald Printshop, 1987.

Ferguson, David S.: *Shipwrecks of Orkney, Shetland and Pentland Firth*, David & Charles, 1988.

Ferguson, David S.: *The Wrecks of Scapa Flow*, Orkney Press, Orkney, 1985.

Gardiner, Leslie: *The Royal Oak Courts Martial*, William Blackwood & Sons, London, 1965.

George, S.C.: *Jutland to Junkyard*, Birlinn, Edinburgh, 1999.

Glenton, Robert: *The Royal Oak Affair*, Pen & Sword Books,

Grant, Robert M.: *U Boat Intelligence 1914-1918,* Putnam, London. 1969.

Hewison, W.S.: *This Great Harbour-Scapa Flow*, Orkney Press, Kirkwall, 1985.

Illustrated London News, October 1939 – March 1940.

Imperial Magazine, 1940.

Howarth, David: *The Shetland Bus*, Fontana Books, London, 2nd Printing 1955.

Korganoff, Alexandre: *The Phantom of Scapa Flow*, Ian Allan Ltd., 1969.

Lamb, Gregor: *Sky Over Scapa, 1939-1945*, Byrgisey, Orkney, 1991.

Macdonnell, J.E., *U-Boat*, Horwitz Publications, London, 1966.

Macdonald, James: *Churchill's Prisoners: The Italians in Orkney*, Orcadian Ltd., 2000

Macdonald, Rod: *Dive Scapa Flow*, Mainstream, Edinburgh, 1993.

Macintyre, Donald: *The Battle of the Atlantic*, Pen & Sword, 1961, 2006.

Marder, Arthur J.: *From Dreadnought to Scapa Flow*, Oxford University Press, 1970.

McDonald, Kendall: *The Tin Openers*, Historic Military Press, Storrington, Sussex, 2003.

McKee, Alexander: *Black Saturday*, Souvenir Press, London, 1959, 1966, 2004.

McKee. Alexander: *The Coal-Scuttle Brigade*, New English Library, London 1973.

Miller, James: *Scapa*, Birlinn, Edinburgh, 2001.

Morris, Keith & Rowlands, Peter: *Exploring Shipwrecks*, Windward, 1987.

Muron, Captain D.J.: *Scapa Flow, A Naval Retrospect*, Sampson Low, London, 1928.

Orkney Library Archives, Folders Reference D1/758; D1/167/5

Potter, John Deane: *Fiasco: The Break-out of the German Battleships*, Pan Books, London, 1970.

Pottinger, J.: *The Salving of the German Fleet*, Stromness Museum, Orkney, 2002

Prien, Günther: *I Sank The Royal Oak*, Grays Inn Press, London, 1954.

Prien, Günther: *Mein Weg nach Scapa Flow*, Deutscher Verlag, 1940.

Prien, Günther: *U Boat Commander*, Tempus, Stroud, 2005.

Public Records Office, National Archives: ADM/1/8428/216; ADM/116/1825-212971; ADM/116/5790; ADM/116/2074; ADM/267/126; MFQ1/895/1.

Ridley, Gordon: *Dive Scotland Volume III*, Underwater World Publications, Twickenham, 1992.

Sinclair, James W.: *Images In Time*, The Orcadian Ltd. Orkney, 1997.

Smith, Peter L: *The Naval Wrecks of Scapa Flow,* The Orkney Press, Kirkwall, 1989.

Synder, Gerald S.: *The Royal Oak Disaster*, William Kimber, 1976.

The Diving Cellar, Stromness: *Divers Guide to the Wreck Sites in the Orkney Islands*.

The Graphic Newspaper, 1939

The Orcadian Newspaper, 1918-1940

The Log of the U47, 15th September – 21st October 1939, (British Admiralty Translation).

Thomson, Douglas: *226 Heavy Anti-Aircraft Battery*, Orcadian, 1996.

Turner, David: *The Ultimate Sacrifice, The World War II Battleship*, Melrose Books, Ely, 2004.

van der Vat, D.: *The Grand Scuttle*, Birlinn, Edinburgh, 1997.

Various: *Diving Guide to the British Isles and Northern Europe*, Swan Hill Press, Italy, 2000.

von Reuter, Vice Admiral Ludwig: *Scapa Flow*, Simon Mills and Wordsmith Publications, 2005.

Weaver, H.J.: *Nightmare at Scapa Flow*, Cressrelles Publishing Co.

Whittaker, Ian G.: *Off Scotland*, C-Anne Publishing, Eyemouth, 1998

Wood, Lawson: *Diving and Snorkeling Guide to Scotland*, Pisces Books, Houston, USA, 1996.

Wood, Lawson: *The Bull & The Barriers – The Wrecks of Scapa Flow*, Tempus, Stroud, 2000.

ABOUT THE AUTHOR

Lawson Wood is from Eyemouth in Scotland and has been scuba diving since 1965. Now with over 15,000 dives logged in all of the world's oceans, he is the author and co-author of a further 45 books. He made photographic history by becoming a Fellow of the Royal Photographic Society and the British Institute of Professional Photographers solely for underwater photography. He is a Fellow of the Royal Geographical Society. Lawson is the founder of the first marine reserve in Scotland and a founding member of the Marine Conservation Society.

This is his second book for AquaPress: the first being the highly successful "Shipwrecks of the Cayman Islands".

ACKNOWLEDGEMENTS

I have always been supported by my wife Lesley in these adventures, an author in her own right; she has great instinct and insight and is a constant source of inspiration. I have been supported by Orkney Dive Boat Operator's Association and many of their members, but would like to give special mention to Kevin Grieve, Jimmy Johnston, George Hendry, and the MV Sharon Rose, Ingrid Thomas, Ronnie Mowatt, Zoe Cairns, Andy Cuthbertson and the MV Jean Elaine, professional and helpful, they have helped me on many occasions, Andy is a superb skipper and incredibly knowledgeable about Scapa and her mysteries; Steve Mowat and the MV Triton; Bob Anderson and the MV Halton; Terry Todd and the MV Girl Minah; John Thornton at the MV Karin; Leigh and Dougie at the Diving Cellar; Sara & Ben Wade, Kieran Hatton and Amy Cromarty of Scapa Scuba. This work would not have been complete without the invaluable help and input from Kevin Heath, Kevin is one of the most knowledgeable people I know on the archival history of Scapa Flow; Bobby Forbes; Ned Middleton; Eleanor at Plainstones; Magnus and Maureen Dennison at Miller's House; Aquasplash Divers; Bristol Scuba Club; Carsten Werner a German Officer and a Gentleman; Northern Diving Group; Ministry of Defence; HMS Royal Oak Survivors Association; R.N. Submarine Archive; Das Submarin Archiv, Wilhelmshaven; Fantasy Prints; Lyness Visitor Centre; Lewis Munro, Curator of the Orkney Museum; Alison Fraser, Sarah Grieve, David Mackie and Kirkwall Library; Public Records Office; National Archives; Imperial War Museum; National Maritime Museum; British Newspaper Library; Historic Scotland; Scottish Natural Heritage; Marine Conservation Society; Lt Cdr Ian Fraser; Reg Rea; Wright & Logan, Cdr I.G.Milne; Orkney Tourist Board; P & O Ferries; Northlink Ferries; British Airways; Richard (Rico) Oldfield; Alan James Photography; Ian Whittaker.

PHOTOGRAPHY

The author's photographs were taken for the most part on the Nikon D100 & D200 digital camera with 10.5mm; 20-40mm zoom; 105mm; 60mm; and 70-300mm zoom lenses. Other cameras used for earlier photographs were the Nikon F801 and F90. Housing manufacture for all of the cameras was supplied by Sea & Sea of Paignton in Devon, Cornwall. Electronic flash is used in almost all of the photographs and these were also supplied by Sea & Sea. These were the YS30 Duo; YS60; YS90 Duo; YS110 Duo; YS120 Duo and the YS350. Additional lighting was supplied by Niterider. Film stock was supplied by Fuji Film and Calumet in Edinburgh. Diving equipment was supplied by Scubapro, except the fins which were supplied by Bob Evans of Force Fin and Stahlsac.

INDEX

APPENDIX IV MAPS AND CHARTS

Admiralty Hydrographic Department Charts

1:30,000	Chart # 0035	Scapa Flow and Approaches
1:200,000	Chart # 1954	Cape Wrath to Pentland Firth, inc Orkney Islands
1:50,000	Chart # 2162	Pentland Firth and Approaches
1:75,000	Chart # 2249	Orkney Islands West Sheet
1:75,000	Chart # 2250	Orkney Islands East Sheet
1:12,500	Chart # 2568	Harbours in the Orkney Islands
1:26,000	Chart # 2581	Southern Approaches to Scapa Flow
1:37,000	Chart # 2622	Plans in the Orkney and Shetland Islands

Ordnance Survey Maps

Ordnance Survey Map # 6	Orkney – Mainland
Ordnance Survey May # 7	Orkney – Southern Isles

Ordnance Survey - Explorer 463, 462, 461 maps
461: Orkney - East Mainland, Ronaldsay, Shapinsay & Kirkway
462: Orkney - Hoy, South Walls & Flotta
463: Orkney - West Mainland, Stromness & Graemsay

Bold figures indicate main entry